INVESTING FOR INCOME

THE RETIREMENT DILEMMA

CURTIS R. BRYANT,
CHARTERED FINANCIAL
CONSULTANT, CERTIFIED
SENIOR ADVISOR

IUNIVERSE, INC.
NEW YORK   BLOOMINGTON

Investing for Income
The Retirement Dilemma

iUniverse books may be ordered through booksellers or by contacting:

iUniverse
1663 Liberty Drive
Bloomington, IN 47403
www.iuniverse.com
1-800-Authors (1-800-288-4677)

Because of the dynamic nature of the Internet, any Web addresses or links contained in this book may have changed since publication and may no longer be valid. The views expressed in this work are solely those of the author and do not necessarily reflect the views of the publisher, and the publisher hereby disclaims any responsibility for them.

ISBN: 978-1-4401-5114-9 (sc)
ISBN: 978-1-4401-5115-6 (dj)
ISBN: 978-1-4401-5116-3 (ebk)

Library of Congress Control Number: 2009930503

Printed in the United States of America

iUniverse rev. date: 7/20/2009

Are you ready to Invest for Income?

Rank the following assets in the order you believe they could be most effective in maximizing after-tax income from your investments.

_____ Tax-free municipal bonds

_____ Treasury notes and bonds

_____ Corporate bonds

_____ Bank CDs

_____ Annuities

_____ Life insurance

_____ Debt-free primary residence

_____ Dividend-paying stocks

_____ Real estate investment trusts (REITS)

_____ Your qualified plan accumulations

See the next page for an evaluation of your answer. Remember that the first four listed above are the most common assets held by investors in retirement.

If you didn't include life insurance, annuities, debt-free primary residence, and REITs in the top six, you need to read this book!

CONTENTS

Forward

Until recently, a high percentage of middle-income people reaching retirement could look forward to maintaining their lifestyles through a combination of Social Security, a company pensions, and small amounts of savings. Now, and increasingly in the future, middle-income people reaching retirement will be dependent upon receiving lifetime income from their savings and/or a lump sum distribution from a company pension plan.

This creates a dilemma, as most people have never managed a significant amount of money without guidance through a pension or 401(K) plan.

Some of the issues with which most people have little experience:

What are the types and severity of risk with which I must contend?
What kind of expectations should I have for investment returns?
How will taxes impact my decisions?
Can I meet my objective without buying stocks?
How do annuities work and can they be useful?
Do I still need life insurance?
For stock market investing, is indexing or active management better?
Should real estate be part of my portfolio?
How can I distinguish a good mutual fund or exchange-traded fund from a poor one?
Should I hire an investment advisor or do it all on my own?
If I am going to work with an advisor, how do I pick a good one?
Beyond basic medical insurance, do I need to provide for long-term care? If so, how?
How do I invest for income rather than capital appreciation?
What does my budget need to be when I retire?

In addition to these personal issues, the financial services industry is just beginning to address this new market. Traditionally, the industry has focused its efforts in two major directions: toward helping clients build wealth and toward helping preserve and transfer that wealth through estate planning.

This was a logical focus in the days when most middle-income people considered retirement income planning unnecessary—or secondary—as they were covered by a company-defined benefit pension plan that took care of their income needs. High net worth individuals and people with their income needs solved tend to manage money the same—regardless of whether they are working or retired. They also tend to focus on "capital appreciation" rather than "adequate income and not outliving their capital."

If the average person reaching sixty-five had a life expectancy of six or seven years, as was the case when Social Security began, the problem would be more manageable with traditional savings and investments. Now with twenty or thirty years of life expectancy at retirement, most old ways of making adequate provision are not sufficient.

Most middle-income retirees in this new world need be more concerned about outliving their money than leaving all they can to the next generation. Those thinking about maximizing what they leave at death are missing the point that the most important gift they can give their heirs is financial independence from them during life. I can't tell you how many times I have had conversations with retired people worrying themselves about maximizing lifetime income if it meant reducing the size of the inheritance they would leave for their children. The new dynamic needs to be: "financial independence first, an estate to leave for the children second."

One factor that makes it difficult for the financial services industry to refocus is that investment advisors and financial firms are usually compensated from fees based upon "assets under management." If an advisor or firm seeks to maximize income and guarantee it will last a lifetime through systematically invading principal using annuities, the asset base for the advisor or firm's compensation from this client is being reduced over time. In addition, only a life insurance company can provide lifetime annuity income—meaning that investment-only firms or advisors are less likely to recommend this procedure. Too often, the advisor is more inclined to encourage taking more risk to enhance income, rather than recommending the safer route of systematically liquidating assets.

Financial firms must develop the skills and capabilities to serve this growing market of income investors. They need to recognize that this new market, though difficult and needing new approaches, is a great opportunity as the number of clients needing their services will grow exponentially. The process for modifying how we approach saving and investing will also be a challenge for the average middle-income earner who wishes a secure retirement.

This book is an effort to provide a starting point in that process. It is not a "how-to" book for the person who wishes to plan without the aid of a financial advisor. It is not a financial advisor's planning tool. It is a sourcebook of ideas for the financial advisor or retired—or soon-to-be retired—individual to use in considering the various concepts, products, and services that may help maximize income and assure it is adequate for a lifetime.

In addition, some chapters will have a small number of "investment nuggets" and a short explanation of why I believe they are true. These nuggets are simply investing beliefs I have stolen, borrowed, or thought of during a half-century in the financial services industry. Some people in the financial services industry may take exception to some of these ideas I call truths. That is okay. Just ask them to explain why they think an idea advanced is not a truth and you should learn much about how they approach their business.

Since each individual has a unique situation, no particular concept, product, or service mentioned herein will be appropriate for everyone. This book neither advises, nor intends to propose, the use of any of these concepts, products, or services.

Facts and opinions expressed in this book are based upon the author's current knowledge and opinions. Since laws, regulations, and markets change over time, the reader should not rely on information in this book without consulting his/her advisors.

CHAPTER I
NOTHING IS RISK FREE

People often say to me "I want something that is risk-free!" Unfortunately, nothing is ever risk-free. As we will see in this chapter: if the principal is guaranteed, the interest isn't; if the interest is guaranteed, the principal is only guaranteed at maturity; if the guarantor becomes more risky, the value of both the principal and interest will decline; if market, business, or prepayment risk goes up, the value of an investment will go down.

Of course, what people usually mean when they say "Risk-Free" is they want something where the principal will not fluctuate in value. The problem is that too many people honestly view that as risk-free.

INVESTMENTS WITH GUARANTEED PRINCIPAL

You can buy investments where the principal sum will not fluctuate in value from a bank, insurance company, money market fund, or the federal government. The tradeoff is the guarantor of principal will retain the right to let the interest rate fluctuate. Those savers with short-term CDs, passbook savings, and money market funds (or accounts) have a guaranteed principal, but from 2000–2004, and again in 2008 and 2009, they saw the bottom drop out of the income it produced.

GUARANTEED INTEREST AND PRINCIPAL

If you buy a product with a guaranteed interest rate for a period longer than daily, the principal sum will not change on your statement—but if you cash out early, the value may be subject to a "market adjustment."

GUARANTEED LOSS OF PURCHASING POWER

Another problem with so-called risk-free investments is that you are guaranteed to lose purchasing power to inflation and taxes. If you look back over time, money is worth 2–3 percent. If you hold it in a cash-equivalent account (a period of one year or less) for a year, the purchasing power of the principal sum will decline by the inflation rate, which averages around 3 percent. Over time, these investments have a yield near the inflation rate or less. To compound the problem, a taxable account will pay federal income taxes currently ranging from 10–35 percent, plus state income tax where applicable, depending upon the income of the individual. In other words, it is not a risk to nominal dollars, but a certainty of loss of purchasing power.

Since cash equivalent accounts, such as money market accounts, generally earn about the inflation rate over time, you can measure your break-even point by dividing the inflation rate by one—minus your marginal tax bracket.

ILLUSTRATION I

MY MARGINAL TAX BRACKET	**25 %**
1 MINUS MY MARGINAL TAX BRACKET EQUALS	**75 %**
ASSUMED INFLATION AND INTEREST EARNINGS	**3 %**
3 % DIVIDED BY 75 % EQUALS YIELD TO RETAIN	
PURCHASING POWER FOR MY TAX BRACKET	**4 %**

To increase the inflation equivalent yield, you have to buy longer periods than one year, or invest in higher credit risks, or in equities. If your marginal income tax rate(s) are more than 25 percent, your minimum break-even purchasing power rate is higher. If your marginal income tax rate(s) are lower, your break-even rate is lower—but not less than inflation over time.

UNDERSTANDING INVESTMENT RISKS

INTEREST RATE RISK is the risk that fixed-income securities you hold will go down in market value because interest rates on securities of like duration and default risk are going higher. Interest rate risk is also the risk that you have securities or savings where the principal is guaranteed at any time, but the interest rate will fluctuate and the trend in interest rates is downward. Having experienced the period from 2000–2004, this should be well understood, but often isn't. From 2000–2003, savers with short-term variable interest rate products saw their income drop below 1 percent from the more usual 3.5–4.5 percent. From 2000–2004, holders of savings or fixed-income securities with maturities of more than one year saw their "market value decline"—though they continued to receive their regular interest. This occurred again in 2008 and 2009.

****

ANECDOTE
During 2002 when interest rates were very low, I was sitting next to a retired friend at our local Kiwanis Club meeting. Financial issues became the subject at our table, and after a while my friend said, "You know, I have always been prudent with my money, not wanting to take risks with it in the stock market or other risky things. I just always put it in CDs or government bonds and lived on the interest. Now I am earning less than 1 percent on my money and therefore having to cash in some of my savings every month! With the amount I have had to cash in, even if interest rates go back to where they were, it won't pay enough to meet my budget, and I will need to keep cashing out my savings. I don't know what I am going to do when it is all gone."
****

Savers and investors seem to struggle more with understanding the concept of market value adjustment in liquidation than they do with seeing their interest income decline.

This risk is called "Market value interest rate risk." It is the risk you assume when purchasing a fixed-income investment that has a maturity date sometime in the future. You bear this risk even if the interest and principal are "guaranteed"—as the guarantee of principal only applies to the value at maturity.

One example would be the purchase of a two-year CD for $1,000 that was going to pay you 4 percent interest annually for two years. The bank issuing the CD guarantees both the principal and interest and, up to certain limits, it may be guaranteed by the federal government. At the end of one year, you will have an asset worth $1,040 ($1,000 X 1.04). When the CD matures at the end of year two, the banker will pay you $1,081.60 ($1,040 X 1.04=$1,081.60). But, let's assume that at the end of year one, you wish to cash in the CD. Your annual report shows a value of $1,040, but when you go to cash it in, they make a "market adjustment" to the principal. They will only pay you $1,030.10. The reason is market rates for one year (you have one year remaining) are now 5 percent. They buy back your 4 percent investment at the amount that would grow in one year to $1,081.60 at a 5 percent interest rate. That amount is $1,030.10 ($1,081.60 / 1.05= $1,030.10). This makes your effective one-year yield on the discontinued CD 3.01 percent. The logic of the bank's position is very clear. When you ask them to cash out your CD contract early, they will only pay you early using the interest rate they could have realized on your money if they were not cashing you out.

If interest rates go the other way, they may pay you more than $1,040, namely $1,050.10 at 3 percent interest ($1,081.60 / 1.03= $1,050.10). This makes your effective yield on the discontinued 4 percent CD 5.010 percent. More likely, they may not give you the premium when interest rates fall as the "market adjustment" gives you a better return for the year than that to which you agreed. So, often with non-traded assets such as CDs, a market adjustment only happens if interest rates go against you during the holding period. With market-traded bonds, the market adjustment occurs in either direction if you sell before maturity.

ILLUSTRATION II

VALUE OF 2 YEAR CD AT PURCHASE	**$1,000.00**
INTEREST RATE GUARANTEED FOR 2 YEARS	**4%**
STATED VALUE AT END OF YEAR ONE	**$1,040.00**
VALUE AT END OF YEAR TWO	**$1,081.60**
ONE YEAR INTEREST RATE END OF YEAR ONE	**5%**
LIQUIDATION VALUE END OF YEAR ONE	**$1,030.10**
MARKET RATE ADJUSTMENT	**$51.50**

The illustration above shows that you assume an interest rate risk if you need to sell before maturity. Generally, the risk is highest when you buy in a low interest rate environment and lower if interest rates are higher. As interest rates rise, market values decline and as interest rates decline, market values increase. Also, the longer time to maturity, the greater the risk of a large market adjustment if you sell early. However, if you are buying a fixed-income asset for income to live on, interest rate risk of the market adjustment type is of little impact prior to maturity. At maturity, however, you do have the interest rate risk that you may not be able to duplicate the income with a new purchase if interest rates are now lower.

SMOOTHING INTEREST RATE RISK

To offset this income risk, many investors buy a fixed-income mutual fund that will buy and hold bonds of varying lengths and interest rates. This will "smooth-out" the risk of falling off the income cliff if rates dramatically decline as they did in 2000–2004, and again in 2007, 2008, and 2009. For those buying a fixed-income mutual fund, a key factor is "What is the average number of years to maturity?" of the assets held by the fund. The shorter the period, the less the interest rate risk—all other factors being equal. However, shorter holding periods mean lower average yields.

A second method of smoothing the interest rate risk is to "ladder" bonds or CDs so that each year a portion of your bonds mature. This allows you to smooth the income being produced as you are reinvesting at a new rate for only a portion of the portfolio. It also allows for extending your average maturity date. This will increase the income being produced while providing for a portion of the portfolio to mature each year in the event of a liquidity need.

ILLUSTRATION III—PURCHASE FIVE BONDS

BOND ONE WILL MATURE IN	**5 YEARS**
BOND TWO WILL MATURE IN	**4 YEARS**
BOND THREE WILL MATURE IN	**3 YEARS**
BOND FOUR WILL MATURE IN	**2 YEARS**
BOND FIVE WILL MATURE IN	**1 YEAR**

AVERAGE MATURITY IS 2.5 YEARS WITH A YIELD EQUAL TO THE AVERAGE OF APPROXIMATELY 2.5 YEAR BONDS.

END OF YEAR 1:
20% OF THE BONDS WILL MATURE AND BE REINVESTED IN 5-YEAR BONDS. THE AGGREGATE YIELD INCREASES AS YOU HAVE REPLACED A 1-YEAR BOND WITH A 5-YEAR BOND.

BY THE END OF YEAR 5, YOU WILL HAVE A PORTFOLIO YIELDING THE BLENDED RATE OF 5-YEAR BONDS PURCHASED OVER THE PAST 5 YEARS.

CREDIT RISK is the risk that the person, company, or government to which you loan money and receive a promise of interest plus return of principal at maturity is unable to meet its obligation. This failure to perform is commonly called a "default."

This default or credit risk is well understood and has had an industry of credit rating companies grow up around the debt market to value the risk. In brief, the way the system works is a credit (risk) rating is established for all large public issues other than federal government debt (which is considered default risk-free). The ratings for one of the rating firms are:

AAA
AA
A
BBB
BB
B

The higher the rating, the less interest must be paid on the security, and the lower the rating, the higher the interest the issuing company must pay. After issue, as the creditworthiness of an issue changes up or down, the rating, and therefore the market price, will go up or down. For example, if an original issue for a particular firm was "BBB"—but with improved creditworthiness after issue, the rating was changed to "A"—the market price for this security would go up. This is because the perceived risk—for the amount of interest to be received and the value at maturity—has gone down. If the rating moved in the other direction, say from "A" to "BBB" the market price for this issue would go down because the perceived risk of receiving the income and maturity value has gone up.

ILLUSTRATION IV

MOVEMENT UP THE RATING SCALE CAUSES THE MARKET PRICE TO GO UP!

MOVEMENT DOWN THE RATING SCALE CAUSES THE MARKET PRICE TO GO DOWN!

CAUTION! As we learned in the credit crises of 2008, rating agencies are usually a good guide, but they are not fail-safe. What a prudent investor does is apply a smell test. Generally, if you find two fixed-income offerings of the same rating, the yield to maturity and safety of principal should be about the same. If there is a difference of more than twenty-five basis points (1/4 of 1 percent) then there must be some significant difference in risk—regardless of the rating. Once you learn what the difference is, you may still judge that the higher yielding offer is preferable, but buying it without learning why they will pay you more is foolhardy.

In retrospect, it seems hard to believe that hundreds of sophisticated financial firms invested in packages of mortgages that included both high-quality and high-risk mortgages primarily because the bundled mortgages carried a AAA rating, paid a higher yield, and "everyone else was buying." In other words, these toxic offerings were rated the same as offerings that only had high-quality mortgages, yet projected a higher expected return. That doesn't pass the smell test for a beginning investor—yet alone a supposedly experienced financial institution. This "herd mentality" frenzy has occurred before, and will occur again in the future! Your job is to ask questions and understand what you are investing in—regardless of what "everyone else is doing"! If you don't understand it, don't invest!

****

NUGGET

The best test of risk aversion is "the pillow test." If worrying about the investment keeps you awake, don't own it.

****

CALL OR PREPAYMENT RISK is the risk that a bond or mortgage may be paid off before the normal time under the agreement. A bond that has this risk should be clearly labeled a "callable bond." A mortgage either has or doesn't have a prepayment penalty in the document. If it doesn't have a prepayment penalty to offset all or some of this risk, it is presumptively "pre-payable without penalty" (callable) by the borrower—usually to the detriment of the lender. Callable bonds and mortgages should pay higher interest rates than those that are not callable as compensation for this added risk.

With a callable bond or mortgage, if interest rates decline, the borrower has the right to pay off the bond or mortgage and get lower cost financing. If interest rates rise, the borrower is locked in at the lower rate. In either direction, the advantage is to the borrower at the expense of the lender. The lender should, therefore, require a higher interest rate at inception to account for this risk.

BUSINESS RISK is the risk a particular company may have difficulty in its business operations that could result in a lowering of its common stock price and/or a decline in its bond rating. This risk may develop from either internal problems and/or external factors. Business factors outside could be, but are not limited to, such things as industry wide over production capacity, environmental concerns, or new competitors.

MARKET RISK is the risk the value of investments may decline because of overall changes in the stock and bond markets without consideration for the intrinsic value of a particular company. This is what we are experiencing in 2008 and 2009.

Stocks traded on foreign exchanges are subject to over-valuation or under-valuation from changes in the dollar vs. the other country's currency. Currency markets are seldom static. Therefore, this additional market volatility in dollar terms needs to be weighed when considering foreign-listed stocks and bonds.

High-tech stocks were overvalued by the market in the late 1990s and may be undervalued today due to their recent fall in price.

****

NUGGET

Markets tend to swing between extremes as the mood of buyers and sellers swing from irrational enthusiasm to irrational fear.
****

INVESTMENT MANAGER RISK. If you are actively investing (by attempting to pick stocks and bonds that will "beat the market," as compared to investing passively through purchase of "Index" or "Asset Class" funds), you have the risk of picking the wrong investment(s) at the wrong time. The downside of this risk is that you can do a little or a lot worse than a passively managed portfolio. The essence of active management is to "beat the market." Since a passively managed portfolio by definition is the average result of all money invested, every dollar by which some managers beat the market in a given year must be offset by managers who trail the market. Finding a manager who will be on the positive side enough years out of ten or twenty to come in ahead of the market averages is pure luck. And, if you hire a professional manager rather than doing it yourself, you pay extra for taking on this increased risk. For more on this subject, see Chapter VIII.

****

NUGGET

Style drift is a major risk for investors in actively managed funds. Regardless of investment style stated in the prospectus, active managers are pressured to move toward what is currently "hot" in order to not lose investors.

CHAPTER II
MANAGING EXPECTATIONS

Those of us who work as investment advisors find one of the biggest jobs we have is helping our clients manage their expectations. Let's spend some time talking about what is reasonable and what is unreasonable or wishful thinking.

NO "GURU" OR "EXPERT" IS AVAILABLE

There is no one out there who can tell you what the stock market is going to do in the immediate future. The investment media anoints a "Guru," "Swami," or "Prophet" once or twice every decade who is said to have special insight into what is going on. This comes about when a stock analyst hits a lucky streak and calls a market turn, or turns, which the rest of the analysts missed. The financial press sees this as a great story that can be hyped, producing a new "market guru." This lasts until he/she blows it—as they always do—by failing to predict the next big market event.

THERE ARE GREAT MONEY MANAGERS

But wait, you say. There have been great investment managers who have beaten the market over ten-year periods, and some even longer. Surely they are ones who stand above the crowd. One who comes to mind is Peter Lynch who, as manager of Fidelity's Magellan Fund, consistently beat the S&P 500 index over a ten-year period, prior to his retirement from active portfolio management. Another name that leaps to mind is Warren Buffett, "The Oracle of Omaha," founder, CEO, and investment manager of Berkshire Hathaway. Warren Buffett is generally considered the most successful investment manager of the last four decades.

All one had to do was invest your money with either of these stars and you would be on financial easy street. But, that is the problem. We learned about Peter Lynch late in his spectacular run. At best, most investors had three years or less to capitalize on what was happening. To have fully capitalized on it, we would have needed to buy in early, and never have lost faith in him until the run was completed. But Peter Lynch was not a wizard when he took over management of the Magellan Fund. He was a young man who earned a big job from his bosses at Fidelity and thereby was given the opportunity to build this track record. At the time, people outside of Fidelity hadn't heard of Mr. Lynch, or if they had, could not know he was a man who was about to set records.

The story is about the same with Warren Buffett and Berkshire Hathaway. Who would have thought decades ago that the most successful investment manager of the twentieth century would be an unknown young man from Omaha, Nebraska? Now that he is elderly and the Berkshire Hathaway stock is expensive, how good an investment is it for a new investor? We have known about Mr. Buffet for decades. Most of us didn't invest long ago. What I need to know is Who are the one or two people in the entire investment business who will set records during the next ten or twenty years? Looking back at past performance does us little good.

The point of all this is, regardless of our fondest wish, the chances of finding the miniscule number of managers who will build records above the market averages are extremely difficult to single out before the fact. Regardless of our fondest wish, we will probably be too late in recognizing the next guru when he first appears. Regardless of our fondest wish, the current investment guru will soon stub his toe, depart the scene, and another will replace him/her. The best investing is to concentrate on building a well-diversified portfolio with a risk profile consistent with our time available and emotional ability to not panic when markets do what markets do. Rather than spend time and money trying to beat the market, it will usually be better to spend time and money building and maintaining a well designed diversified portfolio.

Curtis R. Bryant

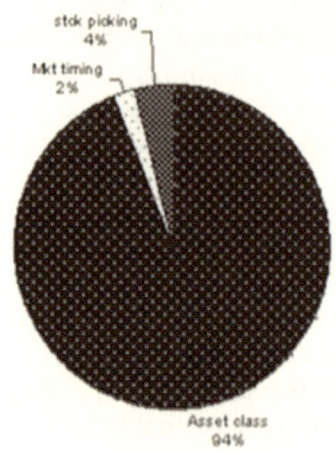

stck picking
4%

Mkt timing
2%

Asset class
94%

ASSET ALLOCATION IS MOST IMPORTANT

A study by researchers at Brinson, Hood & Beebower has shown that asset class selection, or the decision regarding which broad asset classes to invest in, is the most important decision an investor makes over the long haul. Asset class selection was responsible for more than 94 percent of investment results. Picking the right individual securities accounted for 4 percent, and market timing accounted for 2 percent.

For example, we know from historical data that the stock market returns 6.5-7.5 percent per year plus the inflation rate, over time! That means over time an investor 100 percent invested in stocks should reasonably expect to get a doubling of his investment in 7—10 years plus an inflation adjustment in the purchasing power. That is because the "Rule of 72" tells us that investments that return a compound return of 7.2 percent per year will double in ten years. Conversely, an investment that gets a compound return of 10 percent will double in 7.2 years. Since inflation averages 3 percent per year over time, an all-stock portfolio will probably realize 9.5—10.5 percent over time.

In most ten-year periods, fixed-income investments will underperform stocks—but add short-term stability to your portfolio. Therefore, adding fixed-income investments to your portfolio can be expected to lengthen the time it takes to double your investment.

EXPECT LONG-TERM AVERAGES TO HOLD OVER TIME

In bull (rising) markets where your diversified stock portfolio is growing at 15 percent, 20 percent, or more two and three years running, an investor should expect a period when the stocks will wait for the long range 6.5—7.5 percent plus inflation average to reassert itself. Said another way, stocks will probably underperform to bring the averages back in line with long-term valuations. Conversely, if stocks have been underperforming the long-term averages, they will tend to offset this with overperformance to catch up. For example, during the ten-year period ending December 31, 2002, the "S & P 500 Composite Index" had a compound return of 9.3 percent annually. The great bubble of the late 1990s and the great bust of 2000, 2001, and 2002 brought the averages back to the long-term expected range since we had low inflation of around 2 percent for the period.

As this is being written, the stock market has broadly declined from 14,000 to around 7,000, a 50 percent loss. The reasonable expectation is that it will over-perform during the next decade to bring the long-term 6.5–7.5 percent average back. This means a reasonable expectation if you maintain or increase your share of equity holdings will most likely be richly rewarded.

As this is being written, the fixed-income market price has climbed dramatically so that the yields are tragically low for those needing yield. The reasonable expectation is that the fixed-income market will under-perform during the next decade to bring the long–term yields back in line with long-term averages. This means a reasonable expectation if you maintain or increase your share of fixed-income holdings will be severely punished.

An "anchoring bias" causes many investors to assume recent results will continue in the future. Put in simple terms, investors tend to believe what has been happening for the last three years is a good indicator of what to expect over the next few months or years. This leads to investors adding more dollars to the stock market the longer a bull (rising) market runs and selling out or reducing their stocks the longer a bear (declining) market runs. This leads to buying high and selling low—rather than the desired buying low and selling high. A more reasonable bias or expectation is that the markets will revert to the long-term averages over time.

The market timer will say that getting out early when the market starts going down and in when it starts going up will improve this result. But, if you look at the chart below, you will see all you would need to do is miss the ten best trading days in ten years to change your 9.3 percent into 4.2 percent; you should have stayed in fixed-income. There were 2,522 trading days during the ten years. If you were out of the market during the ten best trading days, your return for the period declines to 4.2 percent from 9.3 percent. If you were out of the market the twenty best days, your return would have been less than 1 percent. A reasonable expectation is that you can't time the market and should therefore stay fully invested through both bear and bull stock markets. Data Source: Center for Research in Security Prices (CRSP)

If you can't time the overall market, what about market segments or asset classes? That is even more difficult! The chart below covers the ten-year period ending in 2002 and illustrates the top five performers each year from a group of seven asset classes. It also shows by how much each of the asset classes beat the other. Of the seven asset classes being compared, five were the best performing asset class in one or more years out of the ten, and all seven were at least second one year. Consistently catching the best asset classes is extremely unlikely. What this chart shows is a great argument for diversification and asset re-balancing of your portfolio on a regular basis in order to catch a portion of the top performing asset classes each year.

TOP FIVE PERFORMERS
Asset classes included:
EAFE—Europe, Australia, and Far East Index
L. GRWTH—U.S. Large Growth Stocks Index
L. VAL—U.S. Large Value Stocks Index
S&P 500—Standard & Poor's 500 Largest U.S. Stocks Index
S. GRWTH—U.S. Small Growth Stocks Index
S. VAL—U.S. Small Value Stocks Index
G. BONDS—U.S. Government Bonds Index

1993	1994	1995	1996	1997
EAFE	EAFE	L.GRWTH	S.VAL	S.VAL
32.9%	8.6%	38%	23.5%	38.4%
S.VAL	L.GRWTH	S&P 500	S&P 500	S&P 500
26.5%	2.37%	37.57	23%	33.4%

L.VAL	S&P 500	L.VAL	L.GRWTH	L.GRWTH
23.5%	1.3%	36.8%	22.7%	31%
G.BONDS	S.VAL	S.VAL	L.VAL	L.VAL
11.2%	0.45%	32.6%	14.6%	27.2%
S.GRWTH	G.BONDS	S.GRWTH	S.GRWTH	S.GRWTH
10.3%	-5.13%	29.2%	9.2%	9.8%
1998	1999	2000	2001	2002
L.GRWTH	S.GRWTH	S.VAL	S.VAL	G.BONDS
39.3%	47%	24.9%	22.4%	13 %
S&P 500	EAFE	L.VAL	G.BONDS	S.VAL
28.6%	27.3%	18.5%	7.61%	-6.8%
L.VAL	L.GRWTH	G.BONDS	S.GRWTH	EAFE
21.9%	27.2%	12.6%	0.9%	-15.6%
EAFE	S&P 500	S&P 500	L.VAL	S&P 500
20.3%	21%	-9.1%	-0.4%	-22.1%
G.BONDS	S.VAL	EAFE	S&P 500	L.GRWTH
10.2%	8.2%	-14%	-11.9%	-22.3%

If you look at the next chart, the same holds true. Knowing when growth stocks will outperform value stocks is nearly impossible to predict. In the chart, bars below the line indicate the years and amount by which value outperformed growth. Bars above the line indicate when and the amount by which growth was better than value. Therefore, diversification with asset class rebalancing is indicated.

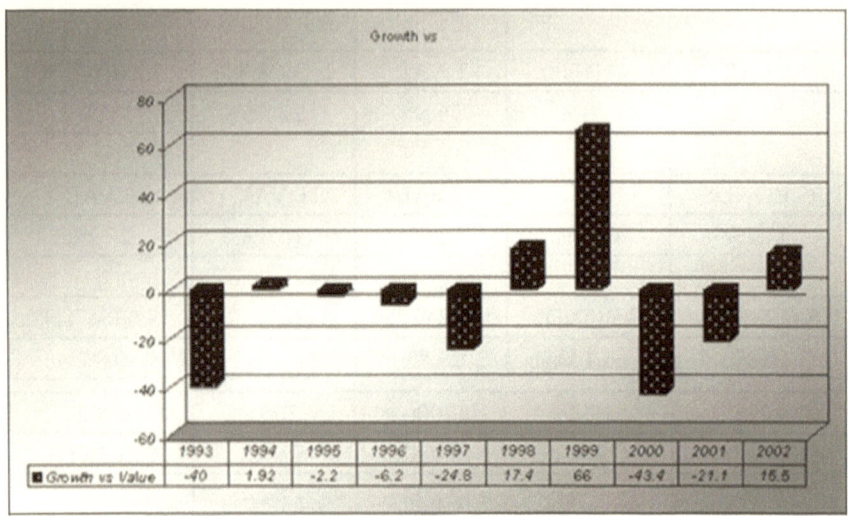

The same holds true in comparing bonds versus stocks. Look at the next chart. You may as well believe you can change lead to gold as to believe you can out-think or out-chart the market in the game called "market timing."

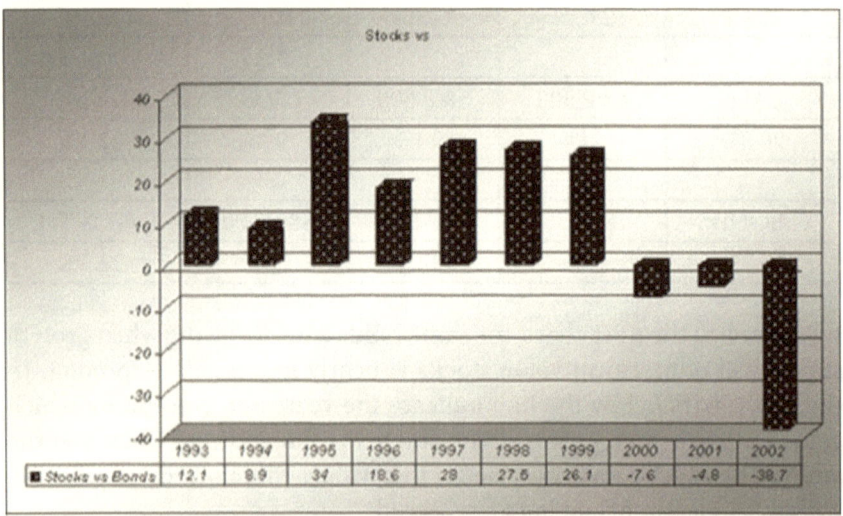

Knowing when foreign stocks will outperform domestic stocks has the same problem.

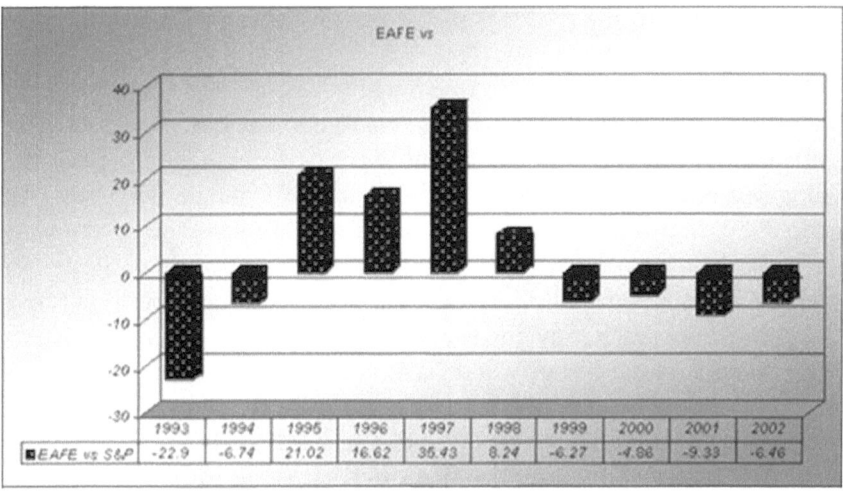

EAFE vs S&P	1993	1994	1995	1996	1997	1998	1999	2000	2001	2002
■ EAFE vs S&P	-22.9	-6.74	21.02	16.62	36.43	8.24	-6.27	-4.88	-9.33	-6.46

DRAWING CONCLUSIONS

- It is more likely than not that my returns over ten years and longer will approximate market averages—if I stay invested throughout the period.
- Selling the asset class which is underperforming in order to buy the one which is over-performing creates "buy high—sell low" rather than the desired "buy low—sell high."
- If I bought the S&P 500 index to reflect the overall market, my investment return would have been in the top half of the seven-asset class returns eight of the ten years (80 percent of the time). Conversely, I could say the S&P 500 underperformed the overall market 20 percent of the time.
- Small cap stocks give me both the best and worst annual returns. This volatility makes it hard to hold them—except as a small percentage of my overall portfolio. Over time, they have an expected higher return than large cap stocks because investors demand more return in exchange for accepting the high volatility.
- In only two years of ten (1994 and 1999) did the five-year government bond have a negative total return. This stabilizer had its best performance when stocks are generally at their worst.

HOW LONG IS "OVER TIME"?

When people like me write about building a portfolio, we constantly say things like "Equities will return more than fixed-income investments over time." It occurs to me that this particular phrase is pretty meaningless without background.

Studies have shown that in any fifty-year period, equities have always returned more than fixed-income. Wow, isn't that exciting! These same studies also show that for twenty-year periods, an equity portfolio will give a better return than a fixed-income portfolio 96 percent of the time. Now that is a workable number. If you are investing every year, each year's investment will have a 96 percent chance of doing better over twenty years if it is all in equities. So, twenty-year periods prove the point! Conversely, any one year's investment has a 4 percent chance (over twenty years)—you would have done better putting the money in fixed-income investments and keeping it there. That tells us that if you invest over a twenty-year period, and hold the investments for at least twenty years, the odds are that only one year's investment (out of twenty) would have been better placed in fixed-income. A reasonable expectation is you will do better with an emphasis on stocks rather than fixed-income.

HOW MUCH STOCK VS. FIXED-INCOME?

In building or selecting your portfolio, however, you should consider that having only equities could be imprudent after your mid-forties. How much in fixed-income? Obviously, there is no set answer without having further facts. I begin from the basic position that up to age forty-five, an all-equity portfolio is generally okay. By age sixty-five, that percentage should be close to 50 percent equities / 50 percent fixed-income. (See "The Bengen Study" in Chapter XIV.) However, personal circumstances and other income sources could lead to modifications. For example, if you have pension income from a former employer that would be considered a fixed-income investment, it could lead to some modification in your equity/ fixed-income mix. You might also have your primary residence paid for. That is like fixed-income equal to what a mortgage payment would be, with the extra benefit of the availability of a reverse or traditional mortgage when your equity portfolio is performing poorly. And, of course, Social Security is a fixed-income benefit and can be put into the equation. Lastly, you have to consider your ability to live with the extra risks of equity investing. I like the "pillow test." If you can't put your head on your pillow and sleep without worrying about your investments, you are taking too much risk.

GREED, FEAR, AND THE HERD INSTINCT!

The studies referred to above assume you invest money and leave it in for at least twenty years. Greed, fear, and the herd instinct will do all in their powers to see that you don't leave the money for twenty years, no matter how you invest it. When the market is hot in equities, you will stay invested in equities, and you will feel pressured to move to more speculative issues, greed. When bonds are outperforming stocks, you will be tempted to switch to bonds, fear. You may even go to cash or money markets. When all people around you are investing a certain way, you will be tempted to modify your strategy, the comfort of the herd.

What this entire discussion is saying is that accumulating the assets for retirement goes well beyond the discipline to regularly deposit money to retirement savings. It requires understanding of how the markets will likely perform over time, the risks you assume with different strategies, and your psychological ability to deal with these issues—both before and after retirement. It also says that those of us who are drawing income from our retirement savings live with the same investment risks as those who are still accumulating. The stock/bond mix may be different, but the need to understand markets and manage our expectations may even be more important as we don't have years to recover from a mistake in judgment.

Wow! You say you're more confused about managing your expectations after reading this chapter than you were before you started. That is good! Most of what you hear about the market or a stock or a fund is pure speculation. What you feel about the direction of the market in the short run is just that—a feeling, not fact. You can only manage your expectations when you know that.

What you can count on is that investors will require larger returns over time from stocks than they will from bonds and other fixed-incomes because they entail more risk (price volatility). Investors will require larger returns from riskier bonds than safer fixed-income alternatives. If a fixed-income security does offer more expected return than a stock, it should be assumed to have more risk than the stock.

Lastly, this is a book about investing for income. When investing for income, you don't want to focus on the market price at which you can sell the investment. You want to focus on the dependability of the income continuing!

CHAPTER III
TAXES AND YOU

Rich people write gigantic checks for income taxes to both the IRS and their state if there is an income tax. However, they don't "pay" for those taxes the way those of us do who are not rich.

Those of us that are not rich pay income taxes with a lower standard of living than we would otherwise have. Let's not get sidetracked with a debate about desirable/undesirable government services, etc. The point is that the vast majority who aren't rich, but pay income taxes, do so by reducing their standard of living now, or in retirement, or in the amount they would otherwise leave to their children or valued institutions.

THE RICH PAY ONLY VOLUNTARY TAXES!

Politicians seem to believe anyone earning $60,000 or more is rich. My definition is that to be rich, a person must have income coming in faster than the desire to spend it—even if they don't work!

If a person is rich according to my definition, he/she will spend for personal consumption the same amount of dollars now, or in retirement, and will leave his/her children enough money to be rich regardless of the size of the checks mailed to the taxman.

So, you say the money still comes out of the rich person's investments. But, does it? When a wise investor considers investing in a taxable investment, they gauge the anticipated return compared to a risk-free investment "after tax." If it doesn't "pencil out"—the investment won't be made. When Ross Perot was running for president, it was reported that he paid little income tax as most of his investable funds were invested in tax-free bonds. In other words, he had made the judgment that the return on tax-free bonds was sufficient to offset the risk compared to the net return on taxable U.S. Government bonds. He also reasoned that currently no other investment could provide sufficient expected return to offset the increased risk plus taxes.

In short, for the rich, income taxes are a voluntary tax. Plus, if they choose to work, it does not change their standard of living, just their activity. If they choose to invest in a taxable investment, it is because they perceive the return they anticipate will be accomplished after tax.

When Steve Forbes was running for the presidential nomination, you may recall that he was advocating a flat income tax of 18 percent. His argument was that the higher tax brackets make some otherwise good investments unattractive and therefore hurt everyone by depriving the economy of its true potential. When asked by a reporter, "But isn't this just a tax break for rich people like you?" He replied, "Don't worry about me. I'll do just fine at whatever tax bracket the government chooses." What he meant was that the income tax I pay is voluntary—in that everything I do is based upon my after-tax return. And if I do nothing to generate taxable income by working, I will still have the same living standard. If I don't invest because of taxes, the losers are the people who would have had jobs in the enterprises I invest in, and the country will be poorer as a result.

Let's assume for example, a rich person with $100,000,000 of investable assets. Typically, that money can be put in tax-free bonds earning 4 percent. That produces $4,000,000 annually with no taxes payable. If I live on $1,000,000, I can still grow my wealth by $3,000,000 (3 percent). To realize the same return on investment, an individual at a 40 percent marginal tax bracket (federal and state) would have to expect a before tax return of 6.67 percent with no greater risk than tax-free bonds. If his tax bracket was 18 percent, as suggested by Mr. Forbes, his before-tax return would only have to be 4.88 percent to realize 4 percent net. This same illustration holds for a rich person (my definition) with investable funds of any amount.

ILLUSTRATION I

TAX-FREE 4% RETURN ON $100,000,000	$4,000,000
LESS CONSUMPTION SPENDING	<$1,000,000>
NET GROWTH IN ASSETS	$3,000,000
TAXABLE 5% RETURN ON $100,000,000	$5,000,000
TAX AT 40% BRACKET	<$2,000,000>
LESS CONSUMPTION SPENDING	<$1,000,000>
NET GROWTH IN ASSETS	$2,000,000

TAXABLE 5% RETURN ON $100,000,000	**$5,000,000**
TAX AT 18% BRACKET	**<900,000>**
LESS CONSUMPTION SPENDING	**<$1,000,000>**
NET GROWTH IN ASSETS	**$3,100,000**

At 40 percent, Mr. Rich will stay with tax-free bonds; at 18 percent, he will move to taxable bonds—thereby giving himself more growth and paying the government more in income tax!

But, you asked, how does all of this affect me? How it affects you is that non-rich people trying to establish financial security must do so with the full burden of all taxes—payroll taxes, sales and other consumption taxes, income taxes, and the reduced economic activity caused by reduced investment opportunities which fail to pencil out. Taxes are not the enemy of the rich; they are the enemy of the middle-through-high earned income group.

So, what can you do? First, always look for choices that eliminate, reduce, or defer payment of taxes. Second, always evaluate return on investment on an after-tax basis. Third, don't assume because there is a tax advantage that it is the best opportunity. Chances are you will not become my definition of rich. But, if you want to become financially secure, you will have to be tax savvy—both while accumulating assets and during retirement. Tax savvy means several things

- Understand that a dollar sent to Washington—or any taxing authority—is gone forever.
- Compare investments based upon after-tax, not before tax, return.
- Take advantage whenever you can of long-term (ten years or more) investments which are deductible, tax deferred, or have tax-free gains.
- Never pass up the maximum "employer match" in a 401(K) or thrift plan.
- Always roll a qualified plan distribution to an IRA, even if the amount seems too little to worry about.
- Take Social Security as soon as you can without losing benefits because of working.
- If you have any outstanding non-tax-deductible-interest debt such as credit cards, pay only the minimum required on the principal of your tax-deductible-interest debt (such as your mortgage) and the maximum you can on the principal of non-tax-deductible-interest debt.

- Refinance your house to pay off any non-tax-deductible-interest debt if the fees and after-tax cost is lower.
- Use any after-tax inheritance to first pay down non-tax-deductible-interest debt.

CHAPTER IV
LIVING ON "FIXED-INCOME"

The concept of living on fixed-income (debt securities) gets much play in the game of politics for both good and bad reasons. For our purpose, the term reflects the concept of developing sufficient lifetime income for retirement, including allowance for inflation, without purchasing stocks.

I am not advocating that everyone should forgo stocks in retirement. Quite the contrary as I think stocks, of the right kind, should be a large part of a retirement investment portfolio. Moreover, academic studies show that the risk of running out of money in your retirement portfolio is greater with a portfolio that has little or no allocation to equities. Rather, my intent is to make readers aware of how to proceed if you elect to use only fixed-income investments. This is not to say this will be a risk-free portfolio. As we saw in Chapter I, nothing is risk free. But, the fact is that fixed-income investments (debt securities) are perceived to be more predictable and stable than stocks (equity securities), which is generally true in the short term. When you are drawing income from your portfolio, rather than building it, this greater perceived stability has increased appeal. Moreover, fixed-income investments' income streams are even more predictable than their total return during any short-term period. In other words, you buy them for the short-term income stream, not an appreciation in value. Therefore, in evaluating between investments of both equities and fixed-income, focus on the dependability of the income stream.

Studies have shown that retirement planning should start with the assumption that your portfolio can produce sufficient income for your needs at a withdrawal rate of 4 percent per year, plus portfolio growth of at least 3 percent per year. In other words, a relatively consistent 7 percent total return. If 4 percent plus 3 percent for inflation isn't enough income for your desired standard of living, your choice will be additional risk, use of annuities for systematic liquidation of principal, or a lower standard of living, now or in the future.

For this discussion we will elaborate on the value of the following investments:

****

A primary residence
Fixed Annuities
Paid-up Life Insurance
Treasury Notes
Corporate Bonds—"Investment Grade"
Corporate Bonds—"Junk Grade"
Convertible Securities
Managed Bond Portfolios

****

YOUR PRIMARY RESIDENCE is one of the safest and most valuable investments you can have in retirement. Ideally, it should be paid for. A mortgage-free home provides you with a 6 percent to 8 percent tax-advantaged return through the reduction of monthly expenses.

Some folks argue it is not a tax-advantaged return as a mortgage payment would be mostly tax deductible. However, I submit it isn't the same as when you are working and making mortgage payments. When working, you are earning a certain amount of income from which you will pay rent or a mortgage. The mortgage payment is often more than the rent would be, but the reduction in your tax bill from the deductible interest usually offsets the difference, plus you are building equity through both payment of principal and appreciation. However, when retired, the mortgage payment requires withdrawal of additional income from funds that would probably have the earnings tax-deferred if not withdrawn. Therefore, you lose. The principal portion of the mortgage payment is not deductible, but the funds withdrawn to pay it are taxable, and the interest deduction is offset by the taxation of the funds withdrawn to cover the interest.

ILLUSTRATION I—MONTHLY

TAXABLE AMOUNT WITHDRAWN FROM IRA	**$1,480**
TAX DEDUCTIBLE PORTION OF MORTGAGE	**$1,000**
NONDEDUCTIBLE PRINCIPAL PAYMENT	**$480**
TAXES DUE @25% ON IRA WITHDRAWAL	**<$370>**

TAX SAVINGS @25% ON MORTGAGE INTEREST	**$250**
NET TAX SAVINGS FROM MORTGAGE INTEREST	**<$120>**
ANNUAL COST OF MORTGAGE ($120 X 12=)	**<$1,440>**

Secondly, your residence automatically adjusts for inflation. Historically, housing costs appreciate at least at the inflation rate over time. In the past ten, twenty, and fifty years, they have appreciated faster than the inflation rate—even after the recent decline.

Thirdly, if both you and your spouse are sixty-two or older, you can obtain a "reverse mortgage" on the property. A reverse mortgage is a non-recourse loan against the equity in your home that may provide either monthly income, an account to tap for expenses, or both. The funds received are not taxable, and the lender cannot foreclose on the loan as long as at least one of the mortgagees remains living there and proper maintenance and insurance are provided. (See Chapter XIII for a more complete description.) So, your residence is a great investment. It meets our objective of providing at least 7 percent annually over time, has little or no default risk if properly insured, and has the added benefit of retaining a probable residual value in your estate—even if you have a reverse mortgage in place. Final thought: if your home isn't paid for when you retire, you may wish to consider a reverse mortgage to clear the traditional mortgage.

****

ANECDOTE

A client we will call Jim, called me in 2002 in a major panic. Jim had done two things in his investment planning which I had recommended against his doing, especially as a retired person. He was hugely over weighted in high tech stocks and he had a full traditional mortgage on his home. His first words were "Okay, you were right about the high tech stocks. Don't gloat, I need your help!" He said he needed to get out of the high tech stocks to stop the bleeding. But his biggest concern was that what was left meant he was going to have to dramatically reduce his living standard and/or go back to work. The solution was we moved his investment portfolio to a much more conservative, income-producing position—plus had him take out a reverse mortgage to pay off the conventional mortgage. This reduced his monthly basic expenses by over $1,500 per month.

Unfortunately, even with these changes Jim and his wife had to somewhat curtail their spending plans and they both decided it would be prudent, though not necessary, to take part-time jobs in order to provide some cushion. Without a reverse mortgage, it could have been extremely painful. As Jim's wife said, "At least we didn't have to sell our home and downsize in a less expensive community!"

If you don't desire to own a property, with all the responsibility that goes with it, you could purchase a life estate in a retirement community. A life estate means you purchase the right to live there as long as either you or your spouse is living. After death of both parties, the life estate is sold to another person(s). You could gain a less stressful lifestyle and possibly reduce your monthly budget in exchange for giving up the ability to have a reverse mortgage—and a residual value for your estate.

FIXED ANNUITY investments in your retirement assets have the advantage of paying more than the 3–5 percent income you could get from Treasury securities or CDs and eliminates the interest rate risk. The amount of increased income over Treasuries or CDs will depend upon your age when you start the annuity. If you and your spouse are both sixty-five, a "joint life-only-annuity" would pay about 7 percent annually. The default risk is almost zero. The disadvantage is that the insurance company does this by liquidating the principal over your lifetime—thus removing any potential for residual value in your estate. There is also no automatic adjustment for inflation, but the 7 percent cash flow allows for setting aside 3 percent for this problem or reducing the amount you take from other investments to buy the annuity.

One way to deal with the problem of this truly "fixed-income" is to invest only a portion of your retirement nest egg in annuities. If good planning says you can withdraw 4 percent annually from your nest egg, but an annuity will pay you 7 percent annually, limit the amount for the annuity to 57 percent of the nest egg (4 / 7 = .5714285). If you have a nest egg of $250,000, 4 percent will provide an annual income of $10,000 to supplement Social Security and any pension income. With an annuity purchased for $142,857 (.5714285 * $250,000) you would get the same $10,000. You still have $107,143 remaining to cover the inflation risk and possibly provide a residual for your estate. To cover a 3 percent inflation risk for the entire $250,000, the remainder would have to grow at $7,500 compounded per year, 7 percent per year ($7,500 / $107,143). Of course, when inflation inevitably increases the need for more income than the $10,000, the purchase of more annuity income will not cost as much as the earlier purchase because you are older (see Chapter V).

ILLUSTRATION II

ANNUAL INCOME FROM $250,000 OF CAPITAL	**$10,000**
ANNUAL INCOME FROM $142,857 ANNUITY	**$10,000**
REMAINING CAPITAL FOR INVESTMENT	**$107,143**
GROWTH OF CAPITAL TO OFFSET INFLATION	**7%**

PAID-UP LIFE INSURANCE can be used to provide tax-advantaged income as well as provide increased assets for investment at the death of the first spouse to help offset the reduction in Social Security that will occur. For full details, see Chapter VI.

TREASURY NOTES & BONDS are the default-free investment available to us all. They usually pay between 3–5 percent interest income. They have the interest rate risk discussed in Chapter I and there is zero protection from inflation. Combined with fixed annuities, they provide a low-risk combination if you perceive inflation to be less of a problem than the 3 percent discussed above. Also, an actively managed bond portfolio often gets substantially better "total return" over time with the tradeoff being an addition of risk. Or, they might be used in a bond portfolio consisting of treasuries plus corporate investment grade and junk grade bonds to enhance return. In short, Treasuries or CDs are inadequate as a sole source of providing retirement income unless you add some level of risk beyond the basic investment.

CONVERTIBLE SECURITIES are both "convertible bonds" and "preferred convertible stock." They have attributes that make them a hybrid fixed-income / equity investment. They both pay dividends or interest that will be somewhat smaller than the interest paid by the same corporation on regular bonds. Both have protection in bankruptcy ahead of common stock. Both provide an opportunity to participate in the issuing corporation's equity appreciation by providing an option to convert to common stock. This can dramatically help us meet our 4 percent plus 3 percent total return objective for the portfolio by allowing significant upside potential when the stock market is doing well without assuming as much risk over time.

Though it is generally viewed as an option to convert to common stock possessed by the investor, you should be aware there can be a "forced conversion" by the company. Generally this will occur when the company wants to reduce the amount of debt on its balance sheet.

Investors holding "convertibles" will be notified of this conversion so that they can take appropriate action, if any.

CORPORATE BONDS (INVESTMENT AND JUNK GRADES) provide enhanced returns over treasuries and CDs because they have more default risk. Investment Grade Bonds are considered to have very low default risk, whereas High Yield Bonds (so called junk) are considered riskier. However, all corporate bonds are by definition safer than the common stocks of the same companies. If a corporation is being reorganized or liquidated in bankruptcy, all bondholders will have superior protection over equity (stock) investors.

In building a fixed-income only portfolio for retirement, corporate bonds, including junk, are very useful. If you need 7 percent on your investments for both income and inflation, you can move from less risky to more risky until you see what risk you must take. This is especially useful if your assets are a little inadequate for your needs or you're looking at providing income through annuities and bonds.

MANAGED BOND PORTFOLIOS provide another way to look at investing in fixed-income securities while enhancing total return. Fixed-income securities have two risks. First, of course, is the default risk. Second is the interest rate risk. Mutual funds do a good job in handling default risk of other than government guaranteed bonds and CDs. What mutual funds don't do is provide a good way to substantially reduce interest rate risk.

Funds are usually "buy and hold managers." They usually buy only one risk layer of fixed-income securities such as "Investment Grade Corporates," "GNMAs," "High Yield" (junk), etc. In recognition of interest rate risk, they will tend to shorten up the holding period when interest rates are low and expected to rise, and lengthen them when rates are high and expected to decline.

The more interest rate risk sensitive approach is to have a portfolio of various fixed-income mutual funds with the intent of moving back and forth among those funds as market conditions warrant, even going to all money market.

Yes, this is "market timing." Though I am a strong advocate of "indexing" where possible and "buy and hold" for common stocks, timing makes more sense when it comes to fixed-income. Fixed-income securities are much less volatile than common stocks. When market conditions change, it is more likely that interest rate changes will have been anticipated for some time, and will only change incrementally over time. This gives the portfolio manager plenty of time to modify his holdings to be aligned with market conditions. Finding and using a good bond manager for part of your fixed-income portfolio may add substantial satisfaction with the results.

****

NUGGET

If you are looking at a fixed-income investment that promises (or has a track record showing) returns equal to or in excess of equity securities, you should consider it riskier than stocks.

RISK / DIVERSIFICATION. When investing for income and evaluating risk, remember that you are more interested in the certainty of the interest and dividends than the market value at any given time.

As with a portfolio that contains common stocks, it is essential that the portfolio be diversified to provide risk reduction. All investments contain risk, but they can be assembled in such a manner that no single event will be catastrophic to the entire portfolio.

LEVERAGE / ARBITRAGE. Too often investors will see the opportunity to take advantage of being able to borrow from one source at a lower interest rate and invest in an alternative fixed-income investment at a higher rate. This practice is called "Arbitrage." The credit crisis of 2008 is an excellent example of what can happen when this practice is widely abused.

Congress, in its infinite wisdom, decided it was a social good to force-feed homeownership to people whether or not they could afford the mortgage payments. To facilitate this objective, they established two "Government Sponsored Enterprises" (GSEs), Fannie Mae and Freddie Mac as they came to be called. These entities are private companies that were established with the market perception that their debt would be federally guaranteed from default. Their subsequent failure and the government takeover of their obligations prove this perception was correct.

By having this perceived default-free status, Fannie and Freddie were able to borrow funds in the open commercial markets at lower-than-market rates for like enterprises that didn't have this perceived guarantee of repayment. In other words, through congressional action, they could borrow almost unlimited funds at low rates because it was government guaranteed, while congress could push a social policy without the messy matter of telling voters that the government was greatly expanding its indebtedness. Both the Clinton and the Bush administrations attempted to control this runaway train, but neither made it a high enough priority.

Fannie and Freddie were free to leverage their market advantage by arbitraging the difference at which they could borrow money and invest those funds in higher-yielding mortgages. In exchange, Congress required that a high percentage of the mortgages that they bought or guaranteed for others were to be what came to be known as "sub-prime loans." These are loans that waive standard qualification requirements of lenders in order to make more mortgage applicants eligible. Because Fannie Mae and Freddie Mac would either buy or guarantee even sub-prime loans, the floodgates of runaway borrowing and debt were opened. At the apex of the bubble that followed, Fannie and Freddie either guaranteed or owned about half of the mortgage debt in the country. When they went belly-up as foreclosures on sub-prime loans began to increase, the entire industrialized world's credit system began to shut down, as there was now no market for much of the world's outstanding debt. Since debt now had an unknown value, banks were seen as undercapitalized and could not extend the additional debt necessary for the functioning of modern economies.

Though there were other factors that contributed to the development of this crisis, it would have been impossible without the congressional intent to increase the level of homeownership beyond what the market would allow when traditional loan qualifications were in place.

Our lesson should be that, when you are dealing with fixed-income investments and someone shows you a method by which you can get "above market rates" without additional risk, you should assume it is a material misrepresentation. It could work out as projected—but the characterization of no additional risk should never be believed.

There was material misrepresentation in the credit crisis of 2008 because of substantial leverage, arbitrage, and reduced standards of credit worthiness forced by the United States government.

Chapter V
ANNUITIES

Understanding the basics of annuities is important to all investors saving for retirement—as well as those who are retired and dependent upon their investments for financial security.

Warning! As primarily an insurance company product, annuities receive no small amount of negative articles in the financial press and in discussions when the conversation is dominated by investment people who are not licensed to sell annuities. This is probably somewhat a carryover from the old days when insurance and investment people were more antithetical to each other than is the case today. It is probably also partly due to a lack of information about annuities because most financial planning people familiar with the subject today see many situations where annuities are an excellent option. In this chapter, we will provide you with the basics so you can determine for yourself what the truth is. The dirty little secret is the fastest-growing segment of the mutual fund business in recent years has been funds sold through variable annuities and variable life insurance policies.

WHAT IS AN ANNUITY? It is a policy (contract) with a company to provide you with an income consisting of both principal and interest payments for a period of time—or for life. At the end of the period—or at death—there is no value remaining. This type of asset is often called a "wasting asset." If you have income from your company-defined benefit pension plan, it is an annuity.

WHY RETIRED PEOPLE BUY ANNUITIES. One reason: certainty of income. Put plainly, there is a major comfort level provided to have a knowable, fixed amount of money coming in each month to cover your basic budget, and which you can't outlive.

****

ANECDOTES

Covering Risk Aversion:

A retired professional and his wife, let's call them Bob and Barbara, who had been long-time investment clients of mine, solved a dilemma using a joint-life fixed annuity. This couple had their home paid for, Social Security, and a very nice investment portfolio to provide them a continuation of their standard of living. This was working quite well as the investment portfolio was not only providing them sufficient income, but showing some net growth to cover inflation.

However, at each of our review meetings, there was a certain tension coming from Barbara about the risk being taken now that "they couldn't replace significant losses with working income." Bob, on the other hand, didn't want to miss growth opportunities from their investments that were 60 percent in various asset classes of stocks and 40 percent in bonds and other fixed-income securities.

After much discussion of the risk/reward features of annuities compared to their current portfolio, the decision was made to invest approximately half their investment funds in a joint-life fixed annuity that would provide, along with Social Security, enough money to cover their current monthly budget requirements. The balance of the investment funds would remain fully invested in the current 60/40 percent allocation to provide a hedge against inflation and a source for special over-budget spending as investment results permitted.

Once this decision was acted upon, Barbara's apprehension went away and Bob could still have fun watching the investment portfolio grow.

Stretching the dollars available:

Some retirees invest in annuities to stretch a money shortage. Nick and Judy had arrived at retirement with savings that would not produce sufficient income at an acceptable level of risk. After considering several courses of action, they solved the problem with a commitment for each to do some part-time work for income—while investing a substantial portion of their investable assets in annuities.

They put half their annuity investment in a joint-life fixed annuity to give them a substantial "base income" along with Social Security. They put the other half of their annuity investment in a joint-life variable annuity to provide income that would ideally grow enough to cover inflation. The balance of their investable assets was invested in a short-term fixed-income investment for their "rainy day fund."

Funding Unusual Issues:

One of the more interesting situations I have seen for using annuities was the situation faced by clients we will call George and Beth. They had Social Security, their house was paid for, they had a reasonable company pension, and a moderate investment portfolio. On the surface, all looked well. However, George's parents had just seen their golden years financially compromised when his father was admitted to a nursing home for care of his Alzheimer's. Other than the Alzheimer's, both of George's parents were in generally good health. However, his mother was not physically able to care for his father, and his father needed twenty-four-hour attention.

The experience with George's parents prompted George and Beth to seek the purchase of long-term care insurance for them. Beth qualified, but unfortunately George was declined coverage except at a substantial extra premium because of arthritis plus his family history of Alzheimer's.

They addressed the problem of providing both of them with LTC protection by first taking out a reverse mortgage on their home. They set it up to provide themselves a partial lump sum plus an income for life as long as at least one of them lived there. They used the income portion to pay the premium for Beth's LTC insurance. The lump sum they used to fund a deferred annuity (to defer taxes on the investment) for George to be annuitized if and when George needed long-term care.

To further understand what concepts prompted them to make this decision, read the rest of this chapter on annuities, plus chapter XIII "Long Term Care Issues."

****

TYPES OF ANNUITIES

There are both "deferred" and "immediate" annuities. These names refer to the date when you will start receiving regular periodic payments. A deferred annuity is one in which the income starting date is sometime in the future. Immediate simply means your income will start immediately, most commonly thirty days following the date of the annuity contract.

Period of Years or Lifetime Payments:

The income period of the annuity can be set for a period of years or for the remainder of your life. If it is an annuity with a lifetime benefit, it can only be written and guaranteed by a life insurance company. This is because only life insurance companies can issue commercial contracts that contain a mortality risk. A "life annuity" is easiest to understand as the mirror image of a life insurance policy. With a life insurance policy, you pay the insurance company periodic premiums while you live and they pay a lump sum to your beneficiary when you die. With an annuity, you pay the insurance company a lump sum (or accumulate it over a period of years) and they pay you periodic payments until you die.

Fixed and Variable Annuities:

A fixed annuity is one where the contract values and income payout are based upon the interest earnings from a portfolio of bonds and other fixed-income investments, plus the length of the payout period.

A variable annuity is one where the contract values and income payout are based upon the changing market value of an underlying stock and/or bond portfolio, plus the length of the payout period.

With a fixed annuity, you have no say in the investment decisions. With a variable annuity, you are given the option as to which investment choice or choices you wish to make from a group of investments selected by the insurance company. This includes the option to put all or some of your money in fixed-income investments.

With a fixed annuity, there is usually a guaranteed minimum interest rate that will be credited to the contract each year—whether you are in the deferral period or the income payout period. This interest rate is usually 2.5–3 percent. Because of low interest rates during the years 2002, 2003, and 2004, and again in 2008 and 2009, this has recently been a real advantage for fixed annuity owners. In most years, it will seem unimportant.

With a "participating" fixed annuity, the company will pay excess interest above the guaranteed rate when earned. In the deferral period, it will simply show up as excess interest credited on your statement. If you are in the income payout period, it will usually arrive as a thirteenth check for the year just ended. If you select a life income payout period, there is no excess interest. This money is used to offset the mortality risk carried by the insurance company.

Costs:

With a fixed annuity, the company makes its profit through a "spread" on the interest they earn compared to what they credit to your policy. This spread is usually in the 1.5–2 percent range. From this spread, they must pay all their costs including commissions to the agent who sells and services the contract and other distribution expenses. This spread is often not spelled out in the contract. You must compare past credited interest to guaranteed interest from past years to tell how competitive the company has been after subtracting their spread.

In a variable annuity, the costs are presented to you as a percentage each year of the total amount of value in the contract. This amount will be deducted from investment performance. This is an additional charge to the expenses of the underlying mutual fund investments that you choose—which also reduces investment performance. You will find all of these expenses explained in a prospectus, which will be provided to you by the sales representative with whom you are dealing. The costs of a variable annuity will be higher than the fixed annuity because it provides you with many more options and benefits. The costs of a variable annuity will be higher than the costs of a mutual fund because it provides you with many more options and benefits. Your task is to determine whether the options and benefits added by a variable annuity add sufficient value to warrant the cost.

Possible surrender charges:

As mentioned above, an agent's compensation and other distribution costs for both fixed and variable annuities are paid by the insurance company from their spread or percentage charged to investment performance. Since all but a few contracts available pay out these distribution costs up front and then recoup them over a period of years, the surrender of a contract may produce a "contingent deferred sales charge" (CDSC). This charge is simply a recapture of the company's upfront expenditures that they have not yet recovered. CDSCs are normally on a declining scale over five to seven years. To clarify, on a five-year declining scale, deposits that are withdrawn after less than one year, would incur a 5 percent CDSC. Money deposited over a year ago—but less than two years—would incur a 4 percent charge and so on down the line. Money deposited more than five years ago would incur no CDSC if cashed in.

The CDSC is levied on the amount deposited, not the earnings. You should check the policy to determine how this is handled as different companies handle it differently. Also, CDSCs are calculated on each deposit rather than from the issue date of the policy. If you are making periodic additions to the annuity, the CDSC may never go away—although some companies will end it after several years regardless of ongoing contributions.

ILLUSTRATION I

YEARS SINCE DOLLARS DEPOSITED:

LESS THAN	1	2	3	4	5 YEARS
CDSC	5%	4%	3%	2%	1%

THERE IS NO CDSC ON EARNINGS AND NO CDSC ON CONTRIBUTIONS THAT HAVE REMAINED IN THE POLICY FOR LONGER THAN FIVE YEARS.

Lastly, there are annuities available that have the option of no Contingent Deferred Sales Charge. Discuss this with your agent before agreeing to an annuity with a CDSC. Immediate annuities have no CDSCs since you begin receiving your income payout at once—after which, you cannot change the terms of the contract. Distribution costs for the insurance company are recovered when calculating the amount of the payout.

Annuity-wrap policies:

There are insurance companies who offer a no bells and whistles "annuity wrap" for a very small annual charge to put around any mutual fund portfolio to make it tax deferred. If you are investing taxable funds that you would like to have in a tax-deferred account, but have no interest in the options and benefits of your more typical variable annuity, this could be a product to consider.

VARIABLE ANNUITY UNIQUE OPTIONS AND BENEFITS

For both fixed and variable annuities, investment gains are not taxed until you withdraw the funds. If you withdraw the funds as annuity income, the underlying cost basis for tax purposes is spread out over the period of the annuity using various formulas. Therefore, the tax is not all incurred up front. If you surrender it all at once, of course, the gains will be taxed in the year received. Plus, if you withdraw funds prior to age 59.5 there will be a 10 percent excise tax levied by the federal government on top of the regular tax. States may also levy an excise tax.

Non-taxed fund switching:

Many investors desire the ability to switch between funds and fund families of mutual funds. When done in a taxable account, these switches can produce a taxable event. Since a variable annuity is a tax-deferred investment, this eliminates the problem.

Deferral of taxes on dividends, interest, and gains:

In addition, mutual funds are required to declare taxable dividends— interest and realized gains made by the fund company in its trading and distribution activity even though the individual investor has not received them. Again, the variable annuity defers all taxable amounts until withdrawal or death of the annuitant.

Annuity death benefits:

Under both a fixed and a variable annuity, there is a death benefit during the deferral period that, for all contracts, equals the higher of the value of the contract or the sum of all purchase payments. This means if you have invested and a market decline or front-end expenses reduces your contract value below what you have paid, the insurance company will make up the difference.

Enhanced benefits at death or annuitization:

Under many variable annuities, you may choose an "enhanced income and/or enhanced death benefit." An example of this would be "for either income payments or death the value of the benefits will be based upon the greatest of 5 percent annual compound increase on purchase payments, or contract value, or the highest annual contract anniversary value prior to age eighty-one."

Additionally, some variable annuities provide a super death benefit where it will pay the greatest of contract value, purchase payments, or 40 percent bonus on the gain in the value of the contract.

Different contracts have different approaches. Some provide only a choice between different enhanced options. Some allow you to stack one enhanced option on top of another. What each provides, however, is an increased annual fee depending on what enhanced options you choose, if any.

There are all sorts of situations where these options may improve your retirement income investment planning. To state just a couple:

- Having a 5 percent compound guaranteed return regardless of investment performance allows an investor to be more aggressive in exchange for accepting a little less upside because of the higher expense the guarantee would cost.
- Having a lock-in of investment gains for the highest five year period means for death or taking annuity income, you can't have a temporary market reversal dramatically alter your plans. For example, an investor in mutual funds who had been planning to retire in either 2002 or 2008 could have had to defer his retirement or accept substantially less money with which to retire due to the crash of the stock market. If the same investor had his funds inside a variable annuity with a "high-five" lock-in, he would have had the same value for retirement in 2002 as if he had retired in 1999 at the top of the market because the 1999 values were locked in. The 2008 values would be the same as 2007 for calculating retirement or death benefits since the 2007 values were higher than either 2008 or 1999.

The income benefit is variable:

The final feature that gives the variable annuity such impact is that the annuity benefit is not a fixed amount, but a formula amount based upon the performance of the underlying investments that you have chosen. This provides the opportunity for the purchasing power of your annuity income to keep pace with, or exceed, inflation. It also makes it subject to downside risk if the market value of the portfolio declines.

MAXIMIZING RETIREMENT ANNUITY OPTIONS

Anyone retiring has the option to take all or part of their retirement funds available in the form of a monthly income for a certain period, guaranteed refund, or life, life with a minimum certain period, or life with a guaranteed refund. If it is for any monthly payout that includes a lifetime guaranteed benefit, it must be provided through a life insurance company and is called a life annuity. Once elected, a life annuity option may not be changed. This is a no-brainer when trying to maximize guaranteed income. You simply take the life annuity based upon your life or your life plus your spouse's. You can choose an annuity based upon your life only; your life only with some certain period, a guaranteed amount paid; an annuity based upon you and your spouse, or an annuity based upon you and your spouse with some reduction at the first death.

HIGHEST INCOME FROM "LIFE ONLY"

As one would imagine, a "life-only" annuity based upon one life with no guaranteed period or amount certain will pay the highest monthly income.

A life annuity for both you and your spouse with no reduction at the first death, and a guarantee of return of principal if both annuitants die prior to full refund will provide the least. This happens because the insurance company guarantees all your money back—plus an individual has a shorter life expectancy than the joint-life expectancy of two people of the same age. For example, government tables show an individual age sixty-five can be expected to live twenty years. Two people aged sixty-five can expect to have one of them live for twenty-five years. To complicate it further, the spouse may even be younger. If the retiring person is sixty-five and the spouse is sixty, the life expectancy for at least one of them is 27.6 years.

So, working with a life and annuity agent, a person considering life income may wish to see if the joint life annuity is the best option. It may be more advantageous to use a single life annuity and protect the second life with life insurance protection on the annuitant to assure the non-annuitant's income after the death of the annuitant. If the prospective annuitant is also eligible for life insurance at standard or preferred rates, this second option may work better.

There are four factors your agent needs to help you determine:

1. Will the annuity income less the life insurance premium provide more income than a joint-life annuity while we are both living?
2. Will the life insurance provide at least as much income to the non-annuitant as would have been provided by a joint-life annuity after the annuitant dies, even within the first year?

3. If the two questions above can be answered positively, how much gain will there be to the insured-annuitant if the noninsured spouse dies first?
4. Are there insurability factors that may affect the outcomes positively or negatively? For example, if the proposed insured were a substandard risk for life insurance, this would make it more likely that a joint-life annuity was the better answer. If the potentially insured spouse was substandard for life insurance, is there existing insurance on him/her that can meet this need?

IS IT APPROPRIATE TO USE AN ANNUITY IN A TAX-DEFERRED ACCOUNT SUCH AS AN IRA?

Many people reflexively say it is not appropriate because the IRA is already tax-deferred, making the tax deferral of the annuity redundant. Yes, it does make the deferral redundant, but as we have seen, there can be many benefits beyond the tax deferral. Not all situations call for annuities. However, people in all situations should check to see if their many features and benefits can enhance the success of retirement income planning.

CAN CREDITORS OF AN ANNUITANT ATTACH THE ANNUITY INCOME PAYMENTS?

Laws change—so one should always check with the insurance company if this is a factor in deciding on use of an annuity. However, the general rule has been that, barring fraud at inception, once the annuity income payments have commenced, creditors cannot get at it. The reason is that the principal sum from which the payments are being made does not belong to the annuitant once the annuity payments have begun. The annuitant has only a right to the income it produces. Further, if the income payments could be attached as received, that would be the same as declaring the principal as subject to creditor claims. It would also present a practical problem in valuation transferable to the claimant since determining the present value of the future income stream on a given individual annuitant would be purely guesswork.

SUMMARY:

*   Annuities are a valuable retirement income-planning tool.

- Annuities have tax advantages and benefit features that are unique.
- Guaranteed lifetime income is only available through annuities.
- Certainty, predictability, and peace of mind provided by annuities perfectly fit the desires and wishes of retired people.

Chapter VI
Retirement Uses for Life Insurance,
Don't Cancel that Policy!

WHAT IS THERE TO INSURE?

Many, if not most, people approaching retirement ask that question unless they have estate tax problems or are attempting to pass a farm or business to the next generation.

Actually, retaining existing life insurance or even acquiring new life insurance can make sense for many people during retirement. Issues such as offsetting the loss of income from Social Security or a pension plan at the death of the first spouse, providing tax advantaged income, or using a policy as a tax-favored part of your fixed-income allocation can all provide benefits that may be superior to the alternative of cashing in the policy and investing the proceeds.

※※

NUGGET

Don't get insurance or investment advice from an advisor who isn't licensed to sell it. Marketing people and marketing companies will always stress the products they sell and downplay the attributes of those they don't sell.

※※

INSURING SOCIAL SECURITY INCOME

Besides estate planning, another reason to maintain life insurance after retirement is for income-planning purposes. For example, Social

Security provides that the spouse of a primary insured will receive one-half the monthly amount received by the primary insured—unless he or she qualifies for a higher amount from his or her own Social Security account. Then, at the death of either person, the survivor will be eligible for just the higher "Primary Insurance Amount." If the primary insured has Social Security income of $1,200 per month, the spouse will receive $600 per month for a total of $1,800 for the couple. At the first death, the survivor's income will become $1,200, a reduction of $600 per month.

ILLUSTRATION I

Social Security benefit of Primary Insured	**$1,200**
(Non-working) spousal benefit	**$ 600**
Total Social Security Benefits	**$1,800**
Benefit lost at first death	**$600**
Survivors Social Security benefit	**$1,200**

If the spouse has his/her own Social Security account paying something between $600 and $1,200 monthly, that higher amount will be lost at the first death. For example, let us assume the lower income spouse has $800 per month earned in his or her own right. He or she only receives the $800—not both the $800 and the one-half spousal benefit. Therefore, the couple's combined Social Security income is $2,000 per month. When either of them dies, the survivor will receive the Primary Insurance Amount of $1,200.

ILLUSTRATION II

Social Security benefit of Primary Insured	**$1,200**
Spousal benefit from separate earnings	**$ 800**
Total Social Security Benefits	**$2,000**
Benefit lost at first death	**$800**
Survivors Social Security benefit	**$1,200**

Each $100 of monthly income lost is like losing capital of approximately $15,000—an amount required to purchase replacement annuity income. Therefore, losing $600 in monthly income is like losing approximately $90,000;—$800 per month requires approximately $120,000 to be replaced. To couples where Social Security makes up a good portion of their family income, this could be a critical issue.

INSURING YOUR PENSION BENEFIT

Many qualified retirement plans offering joint-lifetime payments to a couple also provide the joint-life benefit that may be for different dollar sums after the death of the first spouse. For example, it could be 100 percent of a given amount as long as either annuitant is still living. However, it could be less after the first death, such as joint and 2/3 lifetime coverage; or joint and 1/2 lifetime coverage; or even, no coverage at all for the spouse of the annuitant. The more you guarantee to the survivor, the less you receive while both are alive. The approximate replacement cost can be estimated the same as under the Social Security reduction discussed above.

Obviously, each of these options may have planning advantages. One is to use life insurance to provide replacement income for the survivor when the annuitant dies while maximizing the income while they are both alive. Making this work requires several variables to be effective. Consider (a) What is the cost of buying and/or maintaining the life insurance; (b) if there is existing life insurance in force, how much reduced paid-up insurance will it provide; and (c) if new insurance is required, is there an insurability problem?

FINDING TAX ADVANTAGED INCOME

As we discussed in Chapter III, taxes can be a major drag on your financial well-being. Unless you are very wealthy, every dollar you must pay in taxes will probably be a dollar reduction in your standard of living. Therefore, finding ways you can withdraw spendable cash that won't be taxed is a primary objective of income planning.

If you have one or more participating (dividend-paying) life insurance policies, or Universal Life, which has a cash value, non-rich people will often cash them out and use the funds for other investments. You may wish to rethink that strategy. Your policy could be retained as a "paid-up policy" with a reduced death benefit and may give you the best after-tax return you can get anywhere at the same risk level, plus additional benefits.

UNIQUE LIFE INSURANCE TAX TREATMENT

All premiums can be withdrawn (refunded) prior to any withdrawals being taxable, so-called "First-In / First-Out" (FIFO) accounting.

If you withdraw funds before age 59.5, there is no excise tax.

Earnings can be withdrawn without being taxed through borrowing from the policy at well below effective market rates, and most of any interest paid is credited back to the policy.

An income tax-free death benefit, including any remaining cash values plus loan forgiveness, will be paid at the death of the insured. Effectively, gains need never be taxed!

The section of the Internal Revenue code 7702, which contains the above provisions, is not new, untested law. I have been around the industry since the 1950s and it was the law then. I don't know how much farther back it goes. Suffice it to say, the above should be as dependable as anything can be which involves government rules.

Let's see how this works. Assume you are sixty-five and own a cash value policy for $100,000 death benefit with a cash value of $65,000. Let's also assume your "cost basis" in the policy (premiums paid minus withdrawals) is $40,000. (This assumed policy is for illustration purposes only, as each policy will vary substantially, depending upon a great number of variables such as health at time of purchase, age at purchase, company issuing the policy, the contractual guaranteed interest rate, etc.) I have used $100,000 in order to have round numbers. Any size policy will present the same opportunity.

ILLUSTRATION III

Current surrender value of the policy	**$65,000**
Premiums paid less withdrawals to date	**$40,000**
Taxable gain if surrendered	**$25,000**

The usual option—to cash it in—would be an "ordinary income" taxable event of $25,000 ($65,000 cash value minus $40,000 cost basis). If your combined federal and state tax bracket is 25 percent, you lose $6,250 that cannot be used for your retirement ($10,000 at a 40 percent bracket). You could then save or invest the net, and probably pay taxes on the earnings.

ALTERNATIVE TAX-FAVORED LIFE INCOME

A better option might be to take this money in the form of a life income. There are many optional methods to do this, depending upon your situation. For our purposes, we will assume a life income, male, age sixty-five, with a continuation of payments after death until such time as you and your beneficiary have received back all of your $65,000.

If you did this, the insurance company would pay you $355.55 per month ($4,266.60 per year) for the rest of your life, but no less than 183 months (15.23 years). Some of the payment is a tax-free return of your $40,000 and some is the interest earnings. To oversimplify, for the first 183 months, 61.54 percent ($218.80) of the $355.55 would be tax-free income as a return of principal and the balance would be taxable as ordinary income at whatever your tax bracket is at the time. After 183 months, if you are still living, the entire monthly payment would be taxable.

ILLUSTRATION IV—MONTHLY INCOME

Tax free income as return of principal	$218.80
Monthly taxable income first 183 months	$136.75
Total income first 183 months	$355.55
Taxable income after 183 months	$355.55

ALTERNATIVE REDUCED PAID-UP LIFE INSURANCE

The best option however, may be to take a reduced paid-up policy of $84,000 death benefit (As compared to $100,000 on a premium-paying basis) with the same cash value of $65,000 and the same cost basis of $40,000. By doing so, several good things will happen:

Each year, you can withdraw a tax-free dividend, which will continue to be tax-free each year until you have recouped the $40,000 cost basis. On our sample policy, the first dividend would be $2,353. This equals a return of 3.62 percent tax-free (equals 4.02 percent before tax in a 10 percent tax bracket, 4.83 percent before tax in a 25 percent tax bracket, and 5.93 percent in a 39 percent tax bracket) on the $65,000 cash value. This amount will usually increase each year.

The cash value of $65,000 will increase $840 for another 1.29 percent return on the cash value at the beginning of the year, for a total tax-free gain of 4.91 percent (5.46 percent before tax at 10 percent, 6.55 percent before tax at 25 percent, and 8.05 percent before tax at 39 percent).

In the event of death during the year, your beneficiary would receive $84,000 in tax-free income.

You can leave the dividend in the policy tax free to increase both the tax-free death benefit and the cash value.

The cash value is always available for cashing in, exchanging for a life annuity, or borrowing at a below market net interest rate.

The death benefit amount may be available for tax-free early withdrawal for Long Term Medical Care.

Compare the above to investment in tax-free municipal bonds and you will find it quite attractive—and it doesn't impact taxation of your Social Security or trigger the alternative minimum tax as municipal bonds may do.

ILLUSTRATION V—Annually / year one

Tax free dividend as return of principal	**$2,353**
Cash value increase	**$840**
Tax free return on $65,000 C.V. (4.91%)	**$3,193**
Income tax free death benefit during year	**$84,000**

Assuming you withdraw your dividend the first year, the following year, your new cash value of $65,840 will grow another $924 (1.40 percent) plus the dividend will probably be 3.62 percent of $65,840 ($2,383). The combined tax-free return would be $3,307(5.02 percent) on your $65,840 cash value at the beginning of the second year (equals 5.58 percent before-tax at 10 percent, 6.69 percent before-tax at 25 percent, and 8.23 percent at a 39 percent tax rate). Once again, if you didn't live through the year, your beneficiary would receive $84,000 in tax-free income as a death benefit.

ILLUSTRATION VI—Annually / year two

Tax free dividend as return of principal	**$2,383**
Cash value increase	**$924**
Tax-free return on $65,840 C.V. (5.02 %)	**$3,307**
Income tax-free death benefit during year	**$84,000**

This will go on until the $40,000 cost basis is received through dividends. What happens then? If you "need" this income, it will continue to come to you, it will just be taxable. (It should be noted that policies have a loan option where systematic loans can be used to continue withdrawing funds tax-free. This information is available through the policy contract or by contacting your agent or the company.) If you don't need the income, you can defer receiving it and the death benefit and cash value will continue to increase income tax-free. If you later cash in the policy, it will be fully taxable in the year taken. If you later convert the policy to life income, the income will be fully taxable. If you retain the policy until death, it will be paid to your beneficiary income tax-free. If you use the policy for long-term care, it may be tax-free.

BENEFITS OF A PAID-UP POLICY

- Tax-free income, which should grow each year.
- Increasing cash value available for emergencies.
- Increasing amount available for conversion to life income.
- Tax-free death benefit or tax-free long-term care.

At most times, for most people, growing tax-free income, starting at 3.62 percent, is competitive with bank CDs or Treasury Securities after tax. That being the case, the other benefits are free of charge on an opportunity-cost basis. Paid-up life insurance, bank CDs, or short-term government bonds will not return as much as longer duration—or more risky—bonds or equity investments over time. However, every portfolio needs diversification with part of that diversification being fixed-income when you are in or approaching retirement. For most people, for most times, a paid-up life insurance policy is certainly an option to be considered.

Also, if realizing a better return than the fixed-income policy can provide is desirable, the insured can buy, or 1035 tax-free exchange to, a variable life policy, providing the opportunity to realize equity as well as fixed-income returns and retains all other advantages. Section 1035 is the IRS code section which allows an individual to exchange one policy for another of equal value without having the transaction be taxable.

BUYING A NEW LIFE INSURANCE POLICY

After learning the above, many people ask about buying either a single, or short-term, premium policy in order to gain all of these advantages. Be careful! The government has figured this out, too, and has some modified tax rules for what they call a "Modified Endowment Contract" (MEC). As of this writing, you must have continuing premiums for three years and one month to avoid a MEC. However, if you're going to buy a policy to get the above advantages, be sure you deal with an agent that is knowledgeable. The agent should also be licensed to sell you Variable Life as well as fixed so that you can have an equity option.

****

NUGGET

If you need life insurance for more than ten years, pay for it with before-tax dollars. You do that by purchasing a Universal Life Policy with the premium set at a level that will return all your premiums when you anticipate the need for the insurance will no longer exist.

When you pay a life insurance premium, it is paid out of after-tax dollars. However, the earnings on the cash value buildup are tax-free up to the amount of premiums paid. Therefore, you can get all of your money back and the tax-free earnings will have paid the cost of having been insured. If you die while owning the policy, the beneficiary will receive a tax-free death benefit.

****

DON'T CASH IN THAT POLICY!

Okay, so you still want to get rid of the policy. The traditional method is to simply contact the insurance company, or your agent, and surrender it for its cash value, if any. You may want to rethink that plan.

VIATICAL LIFE SETTLEMENTS

Back in the 1980s, when the AIDS scare was at its zenith, some aggressive entrepreneurs began offering people with short life expectancy an advanced benefit based upon that short life expectancy and the death benefit. The insured received more than the cash value, but less than the stated death benefit. The insured could have use of the money now to help treat his severe illness and the investor could make a profit when the death benefit was ultimately paid. These arrangements were called "Viatical Settlements"

From what we know now, this unregulated experimental concept worked for a while and then became both unprofitable and unpopular as time went by and AIDS victims started surviving their illness. Even so, many AIDS victims and investors did gain from the concept early on.

LIFE SETTLEMENTS

As often happens, this once discredited concept of viatical life settlements laid the groundwork for a much more well thought out program, plus an expansion to insureds who are not judged to be critically ill. Several reputable firms have established a sound business with this revised concept. These offerings are simply called "Life Settlements." A shorthand description is that these companies simply calculate the present value of the projected future death benefit of the policy and, to the extent it is more than the cash surrender value plus the present value of any future premiums, they may make an offer to purchase your policy. Once acquired, they will continue it on either a paid-up or premium paying basis. You receive more dollars than surrendering the policy—and if the purchasing company has done sound actuarial work, they should make a profit.

Not every policy submitted for an offer will be offered a negotiated settlement. Some policies won't "pencil out" for the company to make a profit. Some policies will be too small to be worthwhile even though it pencils out. As a rule of thumb, policies that are most likely to receive an offer will be larger death benefit policies with low cash value relative to the death benefit. Yes, term policies with no cash value can receive an offer! As a matter of fact, one of the better situations for this concept being quite profitable is when a group of large term policies that were purchased to fund a buy-sell agreement are no longer needed by the current owners.

Even if you receive an offer, some people will be hesitant to accept it since it is a relatively new concept. Others may find it disconcerting to have a commercial organization purchase a financial interest in their early demise, although it is only a transfer of that interest from the current beneficiary to a commercial organization. That's okay! The point is to be aware that it is out there and to investigate its potential for you if you are otherwise going to surrender one or more policies.

SUMMARY

1. Retaining a contract with your life insurance company after retirement can be one of the best financial decisions you make.
2. Insuring loss-of-income benefits such as a pension or Social Security can be more beneficial than reinvesting the cash value of a surrendered policy.
3. Converting a policy to an annuity can add valuable tax-advantaged income benefits.
4. A reduced paid-up policy may provide the best fixed-income investment in your portfolio—especially after tax.

5. Even if you still decide to get rid of the policy, a "Life Settlement" may prove superior to simply exchanging the policy for its cash surrender value.

6. With life insurance, there are two basic tax rules that provide the above advantages. First, proceeds paid to a beneficiary are income tax-free (IRC 101(c)). Second, for living benefits, as compared to all other tax-favored assets, there is no taxable gain on income received until all of the cost basis has been recovered (IRC 72(e)(5)(c)).

Chapter VII
A New Look at Stocks

I have always found it interesting that there is a sophisticated risk classification system for fixed-income investments as we discussed in Chapter I, but there is little help in classifying stocks.

There are measures of "Alpha" and "Beta" that can give you some idea as to the price movement of a stock relative to the overall market. I want to know what risk level I am assuming when I buy a stock or a stock fund. Shouldn't there be an easy-to-understand rating system that will let me know if I am making a relatively conservative, moderate, or high-risk investment? Below is my stab at doing that.

RISK CLASSIFICATION OF PUBLICLY TRADED STOCKS

Investment-Grade Stocks

CLASS AAA: Dividend-paying shares that have provided earnings supported dividend distributions for twenty-five years or more and have a price/earnings (P/E) ratio of twenty or less.

CLASS AA: Dividend-paying shares that have provided earnings supported dividend distributions for ten years or more and have a P/E ratio of twenty-five or less.

CLASS A: Shares that have reported strong earnings for ten years or longer whether or not they currently pay a dividend, and have a P/E ratio of twenty or less.

Moderate-Risk Stocks (Potential Winners)

CLASS BBB: Shares that have reported earnings for ten years or longer whether or not they pay dividends and have a P/E ratio of twenty-one–thirty.

CLASS BB: Shares that have reported earnings for five–ten years—whether or not they pay dividends, and have a P/E ratio of thirty or less.

CLASS B: Shares with less than five years of consistent earnings or a P/E ratio above thirty.

Speculative Stocks (Hope over Wisdom)

CLASS CCC: Shares that meet none of the above requirements, have had inconsistent earnings the last five years, but show strong revenue growth, and have a strong balance sheet.

CLASS CC : Shares that have no earnings the last five years, or a P/E ratio of fifty or more, and/or a weak balance sheet or weak revenue growth.

CLASS C: Shares under five years that are publicly traded regardless of earnings and dividends, strong balance sheet, or strong revenue growth.

Gambling
Every traded offering that meet none of the above.

Let's walk through these so we understand the rational of each.

Investment-Grade Stocks

CLASS AAA: Dividend-paying shares that have provided earnings supported dividend distributions for twenty-five years or more and have a Price/Earnings ratio of twenty or less.

Payment of dividends through several market cycles is undeniable evidence of a mature, experienced, and successful business that is the best objective measure of future success. It is undeniable evidence because a company must have generated cash in order to make the dividend payments over time, whereas reported earnings are subject to some level of accounting hanky-panky. Said another way, Price/ Dividend ratios are a better measure than Price/Earnings ratios.

CLASS AA : Dividend-paying shares that have provided earnings supported dividend distributions for ten years or more and have a P/E ratio of twenty-five or less.

Though still very high quality issues, these shares have a shorter record of dividend payments, meaning they have successfully weathered fewer storms in the market place. They also may have higher P/E and P/D ratios.

CLASS A: Shares that have reported strong earnings for ten years or longer, but either pay no dividend or have paid dividends for less than ten years, but have a P/E ratio of twenty or less.

These issues represent very sound companies with good earnings records, but are the lowest Investment-grade issues because they don't pay a dividend, or have done so for less than ten years. Because of this, they won't work as well for retirement income planning and may not get the automatic leverage from the reinvestment of dividends for those accounts that are still in the accumulation phase.

Moderate-Risk Stocks (Potential Winners)

CLASS BBB: Shares that have reported good earnings for ten years or longer, but don't pay a dividend or have paid one for less than ten years, and have a P/E ratio of twenty-one–thirty.

Like Class A shares, these issues lack a long dividend record—and they carry a higher price tag relative to their earnings. A P/E ratio of twenty means you should share in earnings of 5 percent on your investment. At a P/E of thirty, the earnings on investment are only 3 percent. Even if they paid dividends, the dividend would necessarily be below average if purchased at this price.

CLASS BB: Shares that have reported earnings for five—ten years— whether or not they pay dividends, and have a P/E ratio of thirty or less.

Shares of this class are really pricey and are more likely being driven higher than their earnings justify by the belief that future earnings will be much better. In other words, we have entered the realm of Growth Stocks where buyers are making "bets" on future success rather than success that has historic evidence.

CLASS B: Shares with less than five years of consistent earnings or a P/E ratio above thirty.

These tend to be "hot issues." There is some early substance showing in their performance, which has the growth crowd exited. By extrapolating short-term results into long-term projections, it is easy to hype the stock.

Speculative Stocks (Hope over Wisdom)

CLASS CCC: Shares that meet none of the above requirements, have had inconsistent earnings for the last five years, but show good revenue growth, and have a strong balance sheet.

Buyers of these shares are strictly growth oriented. They have divined some new and promising advantage (like new management) which they believe is going to really get things moving.

CLASS CC : Shares that have no earnings for the last five years, or a P/E ratio of fifty or more, and/or a weak balance sheet or weak revenue growth.

These are pure speculation! You get more supportive data at the racetrack from a racing form than you do about the shares of companies in this class.

CLASS C: Shares under five years publicly traded—regardless of earnings and dividends, strong balance sheet, or strong revenue growth.

These are shares that have recently had their Initial Public Offering and are often riding the crest of enthusiastic investors. It will take at least five years before the company establishes any kind of meaningful performance record as a publicly traded company. Until then, stay away! If you are given the chance to participate in an IPO, don't hold the shares long as the initial excitement will usually run up the price early in preparation for a fall to more realistic levels. These are not issues for long-term investors.

Gambling

Every traded offering that meet none of the above. You will not get the 96 percent payoff you would get on a slot machine in Las Vegas!

TRADING STOCKS FOR PROFIT

The period from 1982–2007 gave us one of the longest and biggest bull markets in history. That quarter-century of positive results has led an entire generation to look at making money in the stock market by trading stocks. Investors who were in the market from 1968–1981 didn't think that way in 1981—just as the giant bull market was set to begin—because the market had been flat for thirteen years. Certainly, those in the market from 1928–1945 didn't see trading in the market as a potentially profitable activity as the war ended and the great post-war prosperity was set to start because the market had been flat for sixteen years. No, the advent of widely practiced "day-trading" is a phenomenon produced by our recent and long bull market.

Unfortunately, the amateur day trader appears to do no better than the professional stock picker in beating the benchmark indexes. See chapter VIII below for a full discussion on Indexing vs active management (stock picking).

Even those investors who are not active day-traders are caught in a habit I call "market-price myopia." Myopia is a fancy word for nearsightedness, meaning that you can only see things up close and therefore never see the whole picture. If you can only see a stock from the standpoint of its market price and price movements in the near term, you miss much of the essence of the value of a company. All you see and care about is the market price today and what you think it may be tomorrow.

This myopia leads to "hot stocks," "hot funds," "momentum investing," "a herd instinct," "asset class bubbles" and "buy high—sell low"! Myopia focuses the investor on playing for achieving his/her investment gains solely on market price appreciation rather than earnings or dividends of a stock. It generally leads the investor toward a bias of increasing his stock holdings in a bull market, and reducing his stock holdings in a bear market.

****

ANECDOTE:
I have been licensed to sell securities since 1968. In that time, I have never received an investor call during a bear market decline in which he put forth the argument that he should increase stock exposure.

In that time, I have never received an investor call during a bull market advance in which she put forth the argument that she should decrease stock exposure.

Unfortunately, in all instances where I received a call the above arguments were reverse of the above.
****

BENEFITS OTHER THAN MARKET APPRECIATION

I own my primary residence. Its value to me is one of providing me with a place to live that I enjoy and in which I take pride. In 2006 and 2007, I was told its market value was nearly 2.5 times what I had invested in it. Now, in the fall of 2008, I am told that if I sold it I might be able to realize 1.75 times what I have invested. That is a significant drop in my equity in just one year!

However, at neither the market price in 2006–2007 nor the market price in 2008 was there a reason to sell my home. I had purchased it for the greater value of a home to enjoy and a wonderful place to live. Had I sold it at the top of the market, I would have had to replace it with another home that had the same intrinsic value plus enough lower price to absorb the sell/buy/move expenses. If I sold in this 2008–2009 depressed real estate market, I would still be faced with the same issue. Can I sell at the market price, absorb the costs, and buy something else with the same or greater enjoyment value? Market price on any given date has little to do with my decision to sell and buy a new home since what I am looking for is not connected to price, but enjoyment value.

As an income investor who needs to protect against running out of retirement funds to support your lifestyle, you need to have the same attitude about all your investments as I do about my home. Namely, the price at which you can sell an asset at a point in time is not the issue. Can the assets you own provide what you need (income) both now and in the future at a level that maintains your current lifestyle?

As we saw in Chapter IV, fixed-income investments may be adequate in the beginning, but over time, will lose purchasing power to a combination of taxes and inflation—and likely leave you with inadequate purchasing power in later years. In addition, when we experience periods of unusually low-interest earnings (as we have the past decade), your risk of running out of money will be significantly increased. To keep up, you will need equity investments.

Nevertheless, equity investments don't grow in market value in a straight line. During some periods, they appreciate fast enough to provide both income and appreciation. In other periods, they decline in value. If you count on appreciation of stock values alone to provide both income and appreciation, you are all but guaranteed to fail because the years that decline in value may require you to sell at a lower price than you initially paid. Moreover, once you have sold these shares at a loss, it can never be recaptured because you have reduced the shares you are holding when the inevitable price rebound comes. In other words, you have eaten your seed corn.

As an income investor, your equity (stock) ownership should be in shares that provide both income and potential appreciation! Not only does this support both of your needs (income and appreciation to offset inflation), but, as we learned above, dividend-paying stocks are the safest stocks (Class AAA, Class AA, and some Class A).

THE DIVIDEND ADVANTAGE

Dividends are most valuable from the standpoint that they provide part of the income you need to meet your monthly budget. How much they provide will depend on the price you paid for the stock, or fund, initially. If you buy during a bull market, the price/dividend ratio will make it difficult to have a yield of 4 percent on your equities. However, if you are buying your equities in a bear market such as we are experiencing in 2008-2009, the equity portfolio yield can readily be in the 5 percent or even 7 percent range. Also, if you purchased the dividend paying shares over a period of years, the dividends will likely have increased over time.

THE DIVIDEND STABILITY PER SHARE IS DRAMATICALLY MORE STABLE THAN THE MARKET PRICE PER SHARE.

The stock market price of a given company's stock is set by the collective perception of active investors. I believe this collective perception is primarily set by the emotion of the trading day. During a bull market, most stocks advance further and faster than their individual value would justify because investors are focused on the upward market movement.

They tend to discount negatives and overreact to positives. During a bear market, just the opposite is the case. The more emotional the market, the more uncertain the market, the more the market volatility of prices is evident. That is one reason why investment advisors always qualify their statements with "over time."

Dividends, on the other hand, are set by a company board at a level that the company believes can be maintained in good times and bad. The company realizes that reducing or discontinuing a dividend distribution sends a clear message that the company is having a hard time, which will further depress the market price of the company stock. Market price of the stock IS important to the corporation as it reflects the amount which can be raised per share by floating a new issue. This dividend reduction will not only suppress the stock price, but may contribute to an increase in the cost of borrowing for the company.

This is not to say that, once established, a company will never reduce or eliminate dividend distributions. Dividend distributions are ultimately dependent upon earnings. If earnings go away, or go down significantly over time, reduction or elimination of the dividend will have to happen. That is why you want to concentrate your stock or fund purchases on those companies that meet the Class AAA or Class AA shares discussed above—or even better, mutual funds and Exchange Traded Funds (ETFs) which include only these investment grade stocks. Firms in these two classes are least likely to face the need to reduce or suspend their regular dividends.

CASH FLOW VALUATION

If you own stocks based upon their cash flow from dividend distributions, you should look at a stock or fund's price/dividend ratio rather than their price/earnings ratio, which is the more common method.

With P/E, you say the buyer will have to pay $20 for each dollar of earnings, based upon trailing earnings or upon one-year projected earnings if the P/E is 20/1.

If you are looking, rather, at dividends versus price, you would say a buyer would have to pay $30 to get $1 of dividends if the P/D ratio is 30/1. With dividends, this would always be on a trailing dividend basis—as dividends are usually not projected by management at the beginning of the year.

Another way to measure the value of the dividend cash flow is to give it a market value that can be compared to the current market price to determine if this is a good time to buy, hold, or sell.

For example, if you are seeking a 3 percent cash flow from dividend income, you could convert that to a market valuation of $47.34 per share if the dividend is $1.42 per share ($1.42 / .03 = $47.3334). If the market price is more than $47.34 per share, you would perceive the stock as overvalued by the market. If the market price is less than $47.34, you would perceive the stock was undervalued.

If you have a portfolio of $1,000,000 market value that is delivering dividend income of $51,000, the market is undervaluing your portfolio as you value it based upon 3 percent cash flow. $51,000 / .03 = $1,700,000. If you are valuing based upon 4 percent dividend cash flow, the value should be $51,000 / .04 = $1,275,000

As we discussed in Chapter I, nothing is risk-free. What each of us needs to understand are relative risks. I have not seen studies that address this (though they may exist), so I will take a stab at it, based only on my experience and observation.

RISK OF ACHIEVING INDICATED OUTCOMES
(Ranked from most dependable to least)

U. S. Government Bonds
Government Guaranteed Savings
Life Insurance and Annuities (non-variable)
Investment-grade Corporate Bonds
Investment-grade Corporate & REIT Stock Dividends
Insured "Prime" Mortgages
Uninsured "Prime" Mortgages
High Yield (junk) Bonds
Investment-Grade Stock Prices
Non-investment-Grade Stock Prices
Sub-prime Mortgages and Commodities

This list is neither all-inclusive nor authoritative. My hope is to get you focused on the relative risk of any investment you contemplate from the standpoint of the likelihood it will perform as presented to you. From my viewpoint, for those depending on their investments for their living, relying on the bottom four is very unlikely to turn out as planned.

CHAPTER VIII
INDEXING OR ACTIVE MANAGEMENT?

For the portion of your portfolio invested in stocks, you need to first decide whether you will use indexed or actively managed funds. You could buy individual stocks, but that is usually a bad idea as we discussed in Chapter VII.

AN INDEX FUND is one that seeks to track the performance of a specific group of stocks through replicating an index. The two best-known indexes are "The Dow Jones 30 Largest Industrial Stocks" (The Dow), and the "Standard and Poor's 500 Largest Stocks" (The S&P 500). They are the most tracked indexes by the financial media. All of the stocks in the Dow are also part of the S&P 500.

The Dow and the S&P 500 are often said to "represent the overall market." In market capitalization and in shares traded, this is generally true. However, they only represent large capitalization stocks, which ignore much of the market in terms of offerings available for diversification. A more representative index for the whole market is the "Wilshire 5000" which covers not only Large-Cap stocks, but also Mid-Cap, Small-Cap, plus the most actively traded over-the-counter stocks.

Other common indexes are "NASDAQ 100" (tech stocks), "Russell 2000" (small-cap), and "EAFE" (Europe, Australia, and Far East). There are as many indexes as any one wishes to design. In that regard, we see mutual funds called "Asset Class Funds" which are simply indexes designed by an investment management company to catch a particular market segment specific to a particular diversification objective. Examples include "REIT Index," "Japanese Micro-Cap Index," "Emerging Market Index," etc.

The easiest way to understand an index is that it is a grouping of stocks which tend to respond to overall market moves at about the same speed, direction, and amount of percentage change, up or down, in market value.

In weighting an index, each company is given weight in the index by the capitalization of its market value. If company A stock is worth $1 billion on the market and company B has a market value of $1/2 billion, company A will affect the performance of the overall index twice as significantly as company B.

A NEW WAY TO BUILD INDEXES

In recent years, Professor Jeremy J. Siegel of The Wharton School of Finance at The University of Pennsylvania has put forth a new concept of indexing. Professor Siegel's basic thesis is that "indexes that are built upon weighting the index by stock dividends paid rather than their capitalization value will provide superior performance, over time." His thesis is supported by extensive research, which he discusses at length in his book "The Future for Investors" (see the suggested reading list).

Research shows that this is because dividends are a better measure of the value of a company than is its market price on a given day. Price is simply a reflection of what someone will pay for a stock on a given day and often has little correlation to its earnings value—both now and in the future. For more information, see Chapter VII.

Dividends not supported by earnings really reflect a distribution of capital and therefore cannot long be continued. Dividends supported by earnings, on the other hand, have a much stronger correlation with current and future earnings potential for four basic reasons.

- First, dividend-paying companies are usually older, better-established firms that have stood the test of time.
- Second, management of these companies, in setting a dividend rate, or increasing or decreasing the rate, attempt to set a rate they believe they can maintain once established.
- Third, dividends are hard to manipulate through accounting tricks to make management look like they are succeeding better than reality would indicate—as it takes cash to pay a dividend.
- Fourth, a reduction in the dividend rate per share is perceived as an admission by management that all is not well with the firm.

Therefore, an index built upon dividend-relative performance rather than price/capitalization provides several advantages.

- First, since dividends are much more stable than price, the volatility of "the market" has less to do with the true value and makeup of the index.
- Second, when a general market decline occurs (as in 2008–2009), the automatic reinvestment of dividends provides a contrarian investment by purchasing more shares from dividends when prices are low. This creates the advantage that allows dividend indexes to outperform price capitalization indexes over time (usually ten years or more).
- Third, for those needing income from their stock investments (i.e., during retirement), the dividends paid in cash are a much more reliable way to get the income than selling shares. If you rely on selling shares to receive income from your stock investments, your portfolio will be subject to "reverse dollar cost averaging" as you will be required to sell more shares when the price is down and fewer shares when the price is up. This is a prescription for running out of retirement funds before you die.
- Fourth, dividend-indexed shares will not catch you in a bubble. A bubble occurs when the market price gets bid up on an asset class beyond any relationship to value. This will drive all capitalization indexes in which this asset class occurs upward and create a bubble within the index. On the contrary, market price increases of shares included in a dividend index will result in a relative reduction in importance to the index, as the price/dividend ratio will get worse.

EXCHANGE TRADED FUNDS VS MUTUAL FUNDS

"Exchange traded funds" (ETFs) can be a substitute for "indexed mutual funds." For the purpose of accumulating and then distributing retirement funds, they are not often as cost effective as indexed mutual funds. Most retirement plan contributions for small employers and 401(K) plans are deposited periodically in smaller amounts, distributed in small incremental amounts, and periodically rebalanced to preserve the risk/ reward characteristics of the portfolio. This trading activity is expensive for ETFs as compared to mutual funds because the funds can aggregate all buys and sells for a given day and simply buy or sell what is required in one transaction—for one transaction charge. Each ETF transaction will incur a separate trading charge. This eliminates one of the major advantages (cost) attributed to ETFs. However, at least one ETF family of funds has announced development of a platform for 401(K), which allows for aggregate buys and sells of ETF shares, which may reduce or eliminate this problem in the future.

In addition, for retirement plans that are invested as a pooled account, there could be a cost advantage over mutual funds costs. In that situation, a simple calculation from transaction history can make a determination. During retirement, the favorability of ETFs or mutual funds will be determined by the frequency and size of distributions being made from the fund.

Another purported advantage of ETFs is that there is no tax on capital gains until the owner sells his position, whereas mutual funds must declare gains annually and the owner must pay tax—even if he has not liquidated any of the fund. This is clearly an advantage for ETFs in taxable accounts. Nevertheless, it is meaningless for those retirement funds inside a tax-advantaged investment such as a 401(K), IRA, Roth IRA, Profit Sharing Plan, Defined Benefit Plan, or even a Variable Annuity or Variable Life Policy.

AN ACTIVELY MANAGED FUND is one in which an individual or a group of individuals make decisions about which stocks to buy, sell, and hold for the fund. The objective of active management is to do better than some benchmark. This benchmark is usually an index, or a combination of indexes, which closely parallel the stated objectives and risk/reward of the actively managed fund, or group of funds.

COSTS FOR AN INDEX FUND OR ETF are substantially less than for an actively managed fund of the same class of stocks because there is no expense for research for the index to determine which stocks to buy, sell, and hold for the fund. Another cost savings for indexes over actively managed is from lower trading levels. The difference in cost for stock picking and increased trading is about 1/2 of one percent per year, or higher, on the value of the fund. Some actively managed funds will have lower added expense than 1/2 of one percent due to methodology, size, or other factors. However, one of the considerations that must be made in determining whether to index or actively manage is whether the actively managed extra expense is justified by "value added."

VALUE ADDED can only be determined by performance. It's the American Way to believe that we can do better than average, which is what an index represents. If you buy an S&P 500 index fund, you accept the average performance of large-cap stocks for any given period minus the small fund expense. If you buy an actively managed large-cap fund, you select a fund that will buy only those stocks in the S&P 500 that the manager believes will collectively outperform the average.

ACADEMIC RESEARCH SUPPORTS INDEXING.

In 1990, the Nobel Prize in Economics was awarded to Harry Markowitz, Merton Miller, and William Sharpe for their contribution to the body of work known as "Modern Portfolio Theory." MPT demonstrates that efforts to beat the market are not only unproductive; they are counterproductive because of the expenses that are generated by the required work of active fund management.

MPT tells us an "efficient portfolio" is one that will produce the highest potential return, over time, at a given level of risk (risk/reward). To be able to design and build such a portfolio, we need to determine the factors that will comprise it.

1. First, we must determine an expected (theoretical) return, based upon historical data, for various assets that may be held by the portfolio.
2. Second, we must determine the risk (as measured by price volatility) these assets will likely experience; again based upon historical data.
3. Third, we must determine how these assets correlate. In other words, do the prices tend to move in the same or different direction at the same time, and to the same degree?

One reason we must do "asset-class investing" (indexing) to establish an efficient frontier is that we cannot determine the three factors stated above if we don't do asset-class investing. If you are picking stocks to buy, sell, or hold, even from within an index, your trades will make the data irrelevant; as the historical risk/reward will change every time a trade is made. Obviously, since you are attempting to beat historical and current average returns, your unique mix of stocks cannot be used in building an efficient frontier of risk/reward. If you are investing to beat an average return, but it is difficult or impossible to track the risk you are taking to do so, comparative returns are worthless unless we also know the comparative risk taken to achieve them.

DIVERSIFICATION is the primary method by which investors protect themselves from unanticipated business reversals of particular companies. The average domestic managed stock fund has 134 holdings compared to much larger numbers in most indexes. The S&P 500 of course has 500. The Wilshire 5000 has more than 5,000. Use of index funds will generally provide more business risk protection through diversification than using actively managed funds.

RELATIVE CONSISTENCY. There is no way to reliably select the best mutual fund managers of actively managed funds. Past performance unfortunately does not guarantee future results when it comes to investing. Take the "44 Wall Street Fund," the best performing diversified managed stock fund of the entire decade of the 1970s. If you invested in this fund based upon its '70s performance, you would have been rewarded by holding the single worst performing stock fund of the decade of the 1980s.

PERCENTAGE OF STOCK FUNDS OUTPERFORMED BY INDEXES.

Source: Standard and Poor's Indices versus Active Funds Scorecard, 2nd Qtr. 2003

ILLUSTRATION I

MARKET SEGMENT	5-YEAR ANNUALIZED RETURN	% OF FUNDS BEATEN BY INDEX
S&P 500 INDEX	-1.61%	56.81%
ALL LRG-CAP FUNDS	-1.86%	

ILLUSTRATION II

MARKET SEGMENT	5-YEAR ANNUALIZED RETURN	% OF FUNDS BEATEN BY INDEX
S&P MID-CAP INDEX	+7.14%	92.67%
ALL MID-CAP FUNDS	+2.97%	

ILLUSTRATION III

MARKET SEGMENT	5-YEAR ANNUALIZED RETURN	% OF FUNDS BEATEN BY INDEX
S&P SMALL-CAP INDEX	**+3.72%**	**66.14%**
ALL SMALL-CAP FUNDS	**+2.85%**	

You can pick almost any period and find that more than half of the funds fail to beat the indexes, especially over longer periods. One would think more than half the funds would beat the non-managed average, whereas less than half do in most periods. The ones that do beat the indexes are different in almost every period. Today's winner is most often tomorrow's also-ran or loser.

PICKING WINNERS OVER LOSERS

The illustrations above amplify that one of the considerations when considering indexing versus active management is "additional risk for active management." You pay extra money to have someone pick winners and losers for your fund(s). He or she must, to beat the index, be correct in picking winners and losers; do so consistently over time; beat the index by enough to cover his/her extra cost and profit. Only above that do you gain.

STYLE DRIFT

Another risk for active management is what is known as style drift. Active portfolio managers get compensated by the size of the portfolio they have "under management." Since investors tend to move money toward what is currently hot, the manager is under great pressure to buy some of the hot issues to enhance his results—even if it means moving outside his/her investment style as it was described in the prospectus. Conversely, an index or asset class fund is formulaic. Trading is automatic to the extent needed to adjust to that day's market result. There is no "manager" whose compensation is dependent upon relative performance to another index or another active manager.

These two added risks (judgment errors and style drift) for active management versus passive management mean that, even if the active manager exceeds his benchmark index, he may have failed on a risk-adjusted basis. (If a manager attains after-expenses the same investment return as the index, but exposes the portfolio to more risk to do so, he has inferior performance on a risk-adjusted basis.)

Therefore, we need to use asset-class investing (indexing) in order to build an efficient portfolio. Asset classes work because using them is a "passive" strategy of selecting securities. Once the portfolio manager designs an asset class or picks an index, he or she buys the entire class/index and holds the class indefinitely. Thus, historical return and volatility characteristics can have meaning for the future. Not that historical records can predict future returns and price volatility. What they can do is provide the data from which we can construct a portfolio that will produce the best possible returns over time at a given level of risk.

THE ARGUMENT FOR ACTIVE MANAGEMENT

Regardless of the arguments above, there are a substantial number of investors who will still select actively managed fund(s). That being the case, if I am going to use actively managed funds, what is the best way to go?

Not all active investment managers are good at all types of investing. For example, just because manager A has an excellent track record in picking large cap stocks from the S&P 500 index doesn't mean he/she is equally good at picking small company stocks from the Russell 2000 index. Therefore, you want a fund(s) that can select the best investment managers within the indexes or asset classes that you need to build a well-diversified portfolio.

Active investment managers will have periods in which they surpass the average. They will also have periods when they lag. Therefore, you need a fund(s) that monitor the manager's selected in order to keep or change managers based upon their continuing ability to perform adequately compared to both the indexes and other available investment managers. Active management is a performance business that is in competition with other managers and the indexes. If the manager cannot keep up, or excell, over time the fund must get someone who can.

Another actively managed type of fund to consider would be a "dividend income fund." In this case, the active manager would concentrate on building a portfolio based upon his judgment of the best dividend-paying companies relative to price and value. My personal preference is to stick with index funds (both mutual and exchange

Curtis R. Bryant

traded) because of the cost, judgment risk, and style drift risk mentioned above.

For more information, refer to Chapter X.

CHAPTER IX
REAL ESTATE INCOME

Some people have built much of their net worth and retirement income by buying and holding real estate. As a matter of fact, studies have shown that the two best investment methods for building wealth and providing income are real estate and the securities markets.

Until recent years, investing in real estate meant either being your own property manager or hiring someone to do it for you. This has worked for tens of thousands of investors. The negatives were that you had to be a very astute buyer of property and building a portfolio of properties diversified by geography and type was beyond the capacity of most investors.

Since the 1980s, the securities industry has been finding ways to securitize about every type of investment and trade them on the stock exchanges. The securitization of real estate is what we call "Real Estate Investment Trusts" (REITs). A REIT is a pass-through investment where the underlying trust pays no income tax on its earnings, but "passes through" the income, which is taxed to the investor at his or her ordinary income tax rate.

TRADED AND NON-TRADED REITS

There are both publicly traded and non-traded REITs. Non-traded REITs have a finite life, much as a limited partnership does. The corporate sponsor of the REIT raises funds for investment, manages the property during the holding period, then liquidates the property, and disburses the proceeds. Oftentimes, the liquidation process will be to convert the REIT from non-traded to a publicly traded REIT listed on one of the exchanges.

Publicly traded REITs have an indefinite lifetime. Like any traded security, you buy in at whatever the current market price is, collect or reinvest the dividend as long as you hold the security, and sell it "at market" when you no longer wish to hold it.

REITs usually invest in one type of real estate where they believe they possess some expertise. For example, one may only buy high-rise office buildings. Another may buy only shopping centers. Another limits its holdings to apartment houses. Another may do only mini-storage facilities. There are as many types as there are types of real estate. Therefore, you get geographic and multiple-property diversification within a type of real estate, but to build a fully diversified portfolio of REITs, you must own more than one. Non-traded REITs are usually less diversified than publicly traded REITs.

REIT MUTUAL FUNDS AND ETF FUNDS

A final level of diversification comes from buying a mutual fund or ETF of REITs rather than individual REITs. You can buy mutual funds that are actively managed (trying to pick the best REITs) or an index REIT that buys them all. Mutual funds and ETFs deal only in publicly traded REITs.

A UNIQUE ASSET CLASS

Publicly traded REITs are an asset class of stock. However, compared to most stocks, they receive most of their return from the monthly, quarterly, or annual dividends they pay. Because of this, they often tend to trade more like a bond than a stock. When the market was hot for stocks from 1997–1999, market prices for REITs were cheap since investors were not that interested in what were perceived as piddling returns from the REIT dividends. In those years, you could buy REITs that would generate income in the 10–15 percent range. Growth stocks were gaining 25–50 percent yearly. Today, those same conservative REITs will cost you a price where the dividends will generate an income in the 5–10 percent range. That means the market value of the REITs have gone up just as the market value of bonds have gone up at the same time the stock market and interest rates have fallen.

Two observations: First, if you are an investor building a portfolio for retirement, some commitment toward REITs may make sense as a bond substitute as they provide a similar diversification opportunity as bonds while providing higher total expected returns. In addition, as compared to bonds that have a fixed payout, the underlying real estate of a REIT must increase the amount of dividends paid out as rents increase over time.

Secondly, if you are investing for current and/or future income, REITs provide a higher income than investment grade bonds with a lower risk than junk bonds, and have the added advantage that the underlying real estate should increase the dividend income over time as rents increase.

Like dividend paying stocks of any kind, REITs provide the advantage of reinvested dividends buying more shares when the market price is low and fewer shares when the price is high. This will enhance total return during the accumulation period of your investing. REITs provide higher dividend payout than non-real estate stocks and will enhance your income during retirement.

Chapter X
PICKING A FUND COMPANY

Many, if not most, people give little thought to the picking of a mutual fund company. Like most things in life, there are several contributing factors to this. However, it appears to me that the primary cause is a general feeling that "they are all about the same." Though demonstrably not true, this attitude might be understandable for the investor who has selected carefully an investment advisor, as this is one of those issues you may count on him/her deciding.

In far more cases, I think it is a combination of inertia—plus a lack of understanding—that it can make a major difference in results over time. This is true whether you are accumulating wealth or taking income from the fund on a regular basis. In short, not all mutual funds are created equal!

COSTS MAKE A DIFFERENCE!

Costs associated with owning a mutual fund, ETF, or any other investment, have a profound effect upon the amount you will accumulate over time—or the income you can draw during retirement.

If you save a given amount this year, whether $1 or $100,000, a difference of 1 percent per year will produce a substantial difference in outcome. For example: an 8 percent compound return as compared to a 7 percent return will increase the dollars earned by 16.57 percent in five years, 19.82 percent in ten years, 23.49 percent in fifteen years, and 79.13 percent in twenty years on that one year's savings.

If you are accumulating your retirement nest egg with annual contributions, a 1 percent difference in annual cost can change your accumulated amount significantly. If you are saving a given sum each year, an 8 percent compound return as compared to 7 percent is worth an increase in the amount you have of 3.29 percent in five years, 5.83

percent in ten years, 8.73 percent in fifteen years and 12.67 percent in twenty years! Said another way, if your goal is to accumulate X dollars in twenty years, you can take a 1 percent lower risk per year to get there, or have 12.67 percent more accumulated at the same risk.

If you have accumulated your nest egg and start drawing income for living, you can draw 5 percent on your money rather than 4 percent (25 percent more) and have the same risk in the underlying investments. Alternatively, you can draw the same 4 percent and do it while assuming less risk. That is a not an insignificant reduction in risk of 20 percent.

ILLUSTRATION I
$10,000 AT 8% WILL EARN $4,693 IN 5 YEARS
$10,000 AT 7% WILL EARN $4,026 IN 5 YEARS
   $4,693 / $4,026 = 1.1657% or $667

$10,000 AT 8% WILL EARN $11,589 IN 10 YEARS
$10,000 AT 7% WILL EARN $ 9,672 IN 10 YEARS
   $11,589 / $ 9,672 = 1.1982% or $1,917

$10,000 AT 8% WILL EARN $21,722 IN 15 YEARS
$10,000 AT 7% WILL EARN $17,590 IN 15 YEARS
   $21,722 / $17,590 = 1.2349% or $4,132

$10,000 AT 8% WILL EARN $36,609 IN 20 YEARS
$10,000 AT 7% WILL EARN $28,696 IN 20 YEARS
   $36,609 / $28,696 = 1.2758% or $7,913

Instead of a lump sum compounding at 8 percent rather than 7 percent, it is even more important to look at the gain differential when you are doing annual savings toward your retirement nest egg. The gain reflected does not increase risk—it only lowers costs.

ILLUSTRATION II
$10,000 YEARLY AT 8% = $63,359 IN 5 YEARS
$10,000 YEARLY AT 7% = $61,533 IN 5 YEARS
$63,359 / $61,533 = 1.0297% or $1,826

$10,000 YEARLY AT 8% = $156,455 IN 10 YEARS
$10,000 YEARLY AT 7% = $147,836 IN 10 YEARS
$156,455 / $147,836 = 1.0583% or $8,619

$10,000 YRLY AT 8% = $293,242 IN 15 YEARS
$10,000 YRLY AT 7% = $268,881 IN 15 YEARS
$293,242 / $268,881 =1.0906% or $24,361

$10,000 YRLY AT 8% = $494,229 IN 20 YEARS
$10,000 YRLY AT 7% = $438,652 IN 20 YEARS
$494,229 / $438,652 =1.1267% or $55,577

WHAT ARE FUND COSTS?

I'm going to provide general guidelines here rather than cite specifics. If you are looking at a prospective fund or reviewing one you own, you should check the prospectus and it will tell you their specific charges. You can then check it against these guidelines to see if it is in a high cost or low cost range.

****

Nugget
A prospectus is required by law, but usually is unhelpful to the prospective buyer of a mutual fund. It is not helpful because most investors either don't look at it at all or don't know what to look for if they do.
****

At the low end of costs are S&P 500 index (no-load) funds at around 0.2 percent per year "expense ratio." At the high end are actively managed stock funds with an expense ratio of around 2.5 percent, which includes active management (stock selection), portfolio management, and compensation for the representative who sells and then services your investment. With that large a range, it is imperative to understand what you are paying for so you can determine whether or not the charge is sufficiently justified by the "value added" to make it worthwhile.

INTERNAL EXPENSE RATIOS

Every mutual fund and ETF has an internal expense ratio. The internal expense ratio is the amount that the fund company charges to manage the fund. It is a built-in cost that reduces the gains and increases the losses from the underlying securities.

INSTITUTIONAL FUND COMPANIES

At institutional fund companies, the expense ratio includes basic company overhead, distribution and services expense, and investment expenses—plus any portfolio management expense and a margin for profit. An institutional fund company is one that doesn't market directly to the public. Typically, their expense ratios will average about .2–.5 percent (20–50 basis points) for "indexed funds" and 80–110 basis points for actively managed funds. Therefore, just in basic costs, the difference can be as much as sixty basis points. It is your job to determine if the higher expense is justified by "value added."

RETAIL NO-LOAD FUNDS

At the retail level, no-load funds expense ratios are expanded by about 30–50 basis points from those of institutional funds to provide for indirect marketing to the public. This marketing expense does not include use of a sales and service representative. They market passively through advertising and other indirect methods to make potential buyers aware of their product(s). Added to the wholesale (institutional) costs, this brings the range of expense ratios to 110–160 basis points for retail, actively managed, no-load funds. Indexed retail no-load funds are about 30–100 basis points.

These wide variations are caused by many factors; very large funds should have lower expense ratios; index funds are cheaper than actively managed funds; some provide portfolio management, some don't; bond funds are cheaper than stock funds; international funds are more expensive than domestic funds; and some mutual fund companies are more efficient than others.

RETAIL MARKETING AND SERVICE

If an institutional or a retail company uses salespeople for direct marketing and servicing, that extra layer of sales and service has an additional cost. Institutional fund companies do not bother themselves with this. They simply work with Registered Investment Advisors and the advisory firm determines the add-on expense that the fund company honors by a reduction from the fund, usually quarterly. At smaller invested amounts (less than $250,000), these advisory charges usually start at 1 percent annually. The percentage charge declines to as low as 25–30 basis points annually—depending upon the total funds under management with the advisor—plus the active participation required from the advisor. This means indexed funds purchased through a Registered Investment Advisor will have total internal and advisory expense of about .45 percent (45 basis points) to 2 percent (200 basis points) depending upon the amount under management and the level of services provided. An actively managed fund would be about .5 percent higher at 1.0–2.5 percent. Portfolio management services could add something to these costs, or conversely require high minimum portfolio amounts such as $100,000 or $250,000.

ILLUSTRATION I
RETAIL NO-LOAD INDEX (both Mutual and ETF) FUNDS

INTERNAL EXPENSE RATIOS	20–50 BPS
INDIRECT MARKETING EXPENSE	05–40 BPS
TOTAL	25–90 BPS
OPTIONAL PORTFOLIO SERVICES	25–50 BPS

RETAIL NO-LOAD ACTIVELY MANAGED FUNDS

INTERNAL EXPENSE RATIOS	80–110 BPS
INDIRECT MARKETING EXPENSE	05–40 BPS
TOTAL	85–150 BPS
OPTIONAL PORTFOLIO SERVICES	25–50 BPS

ILLUSTRATION II
RETAIL "LOAD" ACTIVELY MANAGED FUNDS (C shares)

INTERNAL EXPENSE RATIOS	80–110 BPS
ADD FOR RETAIL SERVICES	100–100 BPS
TOTAL	180–210 BPS
OPTIONAL PORTFOLIO SERVICES	25–50 BPS

ILLUSTRATION III
INSTITUTIONAL INDEX FUNDS

INTERNAL EXPENSE RATIOS	20–50 BPS
ADD FOR ADVISOR SERVICES	25–100 BPS
TOTAL	45–150 BPS
OPTIONAL PORTFOLIO SERVICES	25–50 BPS

INSTITUTIONAL ACTIVELY MANAGED FUNDS

INTERNAL EXPENSE RATIOS	60–110 BPS
ADD FOR ADVISOR SERVICES	25–100 BPS
TOTAL	85–210 BPS

OPTIONAL PORTFOLIO SERVICES   **25–50 BPS**

As can be seen from the above illustrations, generally, the least expensive way to acquire mutual funds is to buy "retail no-load index funds." To do so, contact the company directly and buy it off the shelf without additional consultation. Generally, the most expensive will be "load funds." Here we have illustrated "C" shares that can be most easily illustrated alongside advisor fees for institutional funds.

The range of expenses illustrated varies primarily by services provided and the total amount of funds committed to the investment. Also, these expense numbers will not exactly match any actual fund, but are designed to provide an expense range so you can see where your proposed or current fund fits.

LOAD FUNDS

Retail funds that use commissioned sales representatives offer funds through salespeople in what is known as "load (sales & service commissions) funds." These loads usually replace, or significantly reduce, the indirect marketing expense ratio of 5–40 basis points as we discussed for "no-load" funds. These loads, like the above-mentioned advisory fees, will decline as the total sum invested goes up. The exception is "C" shares, which are constant. These reductions in the commission rate, commonly referred to as "breakpoints," are solely a function of how much the customer has purchased through a single fund company.

Note the difference. Reductions in advisory fees are usually determined by the amount you have through a given advisor—even if spread over three or four fund companies, whereas breakpoints in load funds come from the fund company. If your broker had you with substantial load fund investments, you might never qualify for a breakpoint in commissions if the investments were spread among several fund companies. This presents you and your broker with a conflict of interest. The best large capitalization growth fund you determine is with fund company A, but the best large cap value fund is with fund company B. If you purchase both from company A, or both from company B, you will get a breakpoint commission reduction. (The first breakpoint is usually $50,000.) If you buy those you perceive as best, you won't get the reduction.

Your broker has exactly the opposite perspective. A general rule is that if you are working with an advisor, it is better if he is a "Registered

Investment Advisor" so his fees are based upon all your investments—regardless of the number of companies involved. He or she can provide breakpoints in the advisory fee based upon the aggregate of all your investments under management.

MULTIPLE LOAD STYLES

There are several types of commission loads, but the three most common are called "A shares," "B shares," and "C shares."

A shares are distinguished by a front-end sales charge plus an annual service fee of 25 basis points starting in year two. The front-end charge is usually in the 4.5–5.75 percent range for stock funds and usually lower for fixed-income funds. The negative for this load is that it reduces the amount you are getting invested by the amount of the front load. If you liquidate the fund in less than five years, it is a major penalty due to the up-front commission. Some people argue that being locked-in is actually a positive since it keeps investors from switching funds too often, which is a common problem. They also cite evidence that there is no correlation between how well investors do based upon what type of load or no-load funds in which they invest.

B shares are the alternative load to A shares. The representative receives his or her commission up front, but the company doesn't reduce the amount being invested. This means that they advance the commission and other marketing costs and withdraw (usually) 1 percent per year from performance results to reimburse this expense. If you cash out before they have recaptured their advances, there will be a CDSC ("contingent deferred sales charge"). The CDSC period usually runs five–seven years on a declining basis. A five-year CDSC would be 5 percent, 4 percent, 3 percent, 2 percent, 1 percent, 0 percent. If you cash in before one year is up, they will charge a 5 percent CDSC. After one year, but before you complete two years, 4 percent CDSC, etc. After this CDSC period, most fund families reduce the 1 percent annual charge to a twenty-five basis points service fee, which is the same as A shares. It is important to note that any CDSC charges on surrender, for most funds, will only be charged against the amount contributed—rather than the total value of the account. It also needs to be recognized that the CDSC is timed from each deposit. If you purchase a fund with a five-year CDSC, but make additional investments to the fund each year, you will have some CDSC upon surrender—until five years following the last investment.

C shares pay 1 percent annually to the marketing and service people based upon the total value of your fund. C shares have no CDSC, except for money deposited within the past twelve months, which is usually 1 percent because they have expended this money up front to the marketing and service people and will recoup it during the year. Many companies reduce the CDSC effect by paying the marketing and service people 1/4 of 1 percent at the beginning of each quarter. The registered representative (broker) will receive a portion of the 1 percent each year you retain the fund investment, and it will be calculated on the total value—including gains and losses. This better aligns the objectives of the representative with the investor. The better the investment turns out, the better both parties do. In short, C shares are somewhat like fees for Registered Investment Advisors—although on larger sums, the C shares charge can become excessive and should be changed to fees.

ADVANTAGES OF A AND B SHARES

Both A and B shares have the advantage of making it profitable for salespeople to sell smaller amounts. If you want to invest only $10,000 in a fund, the marketing charge will amount to $450–575 dollars for a stock fund, and somewhat less for a bond fund. You would then pay a .25 percent, ($25 on $10,000) annual service charge. The same is true for B shares—though they are structured differently. On the other hand, your marketing charge under C shares in year one would only be $100 on the $10,000. This makes it impractical for a representative to complete the marketing and application process unless the marketing is being done on a group basis such as when enrolling a 401(K) plan.

It is also important to realize that the retail marketer you work with doesn't get all of the marketing charge you pay. A portion of it goes to a "broker-dealer," as required by law. The broker-dealer is responsible for training and supervising this person. This revenue sharing by the broker-dealer can be in the 10–50 percent range—depending upon the level of services provided to the representative by the broker-dealer.

WRAP FEES

Another way of paying for marketing, services, and advisory activity is the use of a "wrap account." They appear similar to fees for a Registered Investment Advisor—although they are not. A Registered Investment Advisor is independent of product providers and adds his fee to the costs of the underlying investments with which he assists you. With a wrap fee, you are usually purchasing all services from a single firm and they "wrap" all the various layers of expenses into one fee, which is a percentage of assets under management. Your advisor for a wrap account is often an employee of the company. The investment manager is an employee of the company. The people executing the actual trades are employees of the company. With a wrap fee system, you are buying into the way the company does things—it is all or nothing. By contrast, an independent investment advisor can help select services from companies in which he has no vested interest as an employee. With a wrap account, you will usually, but not always, have options only from that one company's offerings.

WHAT DO YOU WANT A FUND COMPANY TO DO FOR YOU?

I want a fund company who will provide products at a competitive price.

I want a company who either uses index funds or, for actively managed accounts, contracts and monitors sub-advisors who provide the actual investment decisions within assigned parameters. These sub-advisors can more readily be changed than can employees of the fund company.

I want a fund company who is not in any other financial service that might create conflicts of interest. For example, if the firm is also involved with IPOs (Initial Public Offerings) or making markets in particular issues, I don't want to own one of their mutual funds because they do not have an objective view of these stocks. Additionally, the company profits by having the company's mutual fund buy these stocks.

I don't want to buy a fund from a company salesman/employee. This is because there is pressure—sometimes direct pressure—to sell the employer's fund—even if it is not demonstratively the best product available for your objectives.

SUMMARY

- Expenses associated with buying and holding mutual funds can have a major impact upon outcomes.
- Actively managed funds are more expensive than index funds and need to be compared on a risk-adjusted basis. For more information, refer to Chapter VIII.
- How you pay a broker or Investment Advisor can make a difference in the cost/benefit of their services.

- All charges need to be evaluated on a cost/benefit basis.
- Large fund families always have a currently competitive product because they have a product in all market classes. If you depend upon advertising to attract investors, you must have something in the hot market of the day to attract that new money.
- There are several types of load funds. The least understood is the "dummy load." A dummy load is one where they try to convince you there is no marketing expense. A "no-load" fund simply means the firm will not add on anything for a retail representative to sell and service their products. They will still charge for their direct marketing and ongoing service. You just don't see it as a separate expense.
- No active-management investment firm is good in all investment classes. That is just a fact. One firm may be particularly good with one asset class, such as large capitalization U.S. stocks or corporate bonds. It does not mean they are good in the others. Evidence indicates the opposite is true. What does that tell you about wrap accounts?
- The typical investor moves from fund to fund about every two–three years—usually chasing the "hot fund." This is especially true with no-load funds. Over ten year and longer periods, every fund will have better and worse periods as their style goes in and out of favor in the market. That is when many investors move to another fund, which is pricey because their style is currently doing well. Sell low, buy high anyone?

Chapter XI
WHY HAVE AN ADVISOR?

Reasonable people can have differences of opinion about their overall investment objectives. Some will say, "I want to achieve market returns." Others may say, "I want to do better than the market." Yet others may say, "I want to do better than I can get from a savings account, but I want to protect myself from losing what I have." We also hear "I'm not counting on this money so I want to see how well we can do."

Regardless of your perspective, the question is Do you have the knowledge and judgment to manage the funds, or the time, interest, and commitment to acquire what it takes to do the job on your own? This isn't rocket science. On the other hand, studies show most investors don't come close to getting market returns, let alone beating the market.

UNDERSTANDING MARKET RETURNS

But, isn't it true that market returns are the average of what all investors realize? Aren't half the investors equaling or beating the market? Unfortunately, the answer is no! The average of the market is the "average return on the amount of dollars invested," not the return realized by the average investor.

So, what does the average investor realize? Dalbar, a recognized research firm on investing, tells us that from January 1984 through December 2005, the S&P 500 stock index had a compound growth rate of 13.2 percent—whereas the average equity fund investor realized only 3.7 percent compound return.

But, it isn't just investors in the stock market. The Long Term Government Bond Index for the same period realized a compound return of 5.7 percent whereas the average fixed-income investor realized only 2 percent.

Based upon this and other studies, it appears the objective for most investors shouldn't be to beat the market averages, but to hope for closer-to-market returns than the average investor.

HOW CAN THIS BE?

What do investors do that makes them so dramatically under-perform the market average?

Published market averages for any period assume all dollars are in at the start of the period and remain invested for the entire period. Most individual investors are contributing money, withdrawing money, changing allocations, switching funds, or some combination of all four during the period. Therefore, how much is contributed, withdrawn, or reallocated or switched, and when will determine the variance from the market averages.

BUY HIGH—SELL LOW

Analysis of the market indicates that investors increase the amount going to a particular investment as prices rise and withdraw money when prices are declining. It further shows that the higher the prices get, the more money investors will direct to that investment; the lower they get, the more they will sell, or at least stop buying!

This turns the basic supply/demand equation on its head by increasing demand because the price goes up and decreasing demand because the price is declining. If the average investor were acting rationally, he/she would be selling shares when prices are increasing and buying shares as prices are declining.

BASIC ECONOMICS STILL WORKS

Of course, the price result of demand for more shares fits the basic understanding of supply/demand relationships. As demand for a given investment goes up, the price will go up—unless supply (willing sellers) can be increased. Conversely, as the demand for a given investment declines, the price will decline—unless supply goes down.

Remember, in any perfect market, the price will move up or down until you balance the number of willing buyers with willing sellers at the market-clearing price.

If you are a corn farmer, when the price you can get for your corn is too low, you put as much as you can of it in a silo rather than sell it, thereby reducing supply that would otherwise be available, and slowing further price decline. In another year—when the price is high—you will sell both the current year's production and the corn you have in the silo—thereby increasing the supply, which will moderate further price increases. If you run a feedlot for cattle, you will undoubtedly do the opposite and buy ahead of your needs when prices are low and use those stored supplies when the prices are high. Both these players will instinctively help the market find its clearing price on any given day.

Likewise, oil well production and sales into the market will respond to the prices being offered. When prices are low, the less productive wells will be "closed in" and their production never offered to the market as it will cost the producer more than he can sell it for. When prices are high, every well whose production can be sold profitably will be operating. Though users of petroleum products may not be able to adjust their demand as readily as producers can adjust the supply, marginal uses will be curtailed or postponed as the market price increases. Demand will increase as prices fall, and prices will go up and down until the market-clearing price is achieved.

Unfortunately, the average investor acts counter to this logical response to changing market prices. He or she, unfortunately, increases the demand for investments by purchasing what is increasing in price, and increases supply by selling what is stagnant or declining in price. This is true of not only stocks, but also bonds, real estate, precious gems, gold, pork bellies, wheat, mutual funds, etc. In other words, the average investor's natural instinct is to do the opposite of that which will create the best returns. This contrasts starkly with the actions of producers and consumers of products.

Almost everyone I talk to can readily quote the basic rule of investing: buy low—sell high. However, if the typical investor is following his natural instinct, the result will be to buy high—sell low.

"ANCHORING BIAS" IS THE CULPRIT!

Investors who have structured diversified portfolios—as they should— often modify their asset allocations every two–four years to adjust their portfolios to what has been doing well in the past three years. This is caused by what academics who study the psychology of investing call "anchoring bias." The subconscious belief that what has been happening over the last three years is "normal" and therefore likely to continue.

These investors sell the asset classes that are doing poorly, or even less well, in order to purchase the asset classes that are outperforming their expected returns. This accomplishes two things. First, it sells low and buys high! Second, it virtually assures that the investor will underperform the market averages over a ten-year period.

WHAT CAN BE DONE ABOUT IT?

The most basic thing to do is to be well diversified so that when one type of investment you own is going down, another is going up. This reduces the instinctive pressure to sell the declining asset(s) and invest in the appreciating asset(s). This diversified aggregate return should keep your overall return close to published overall market averages. However, it must be expected that any diversified portfolio will have short-term periods when it underperforms market averages.

The next best thing is to periodically "rebalance" this diversified portfolio. Most experts suggest no less than once each year. I prefer quarterly. This automatic buying and selling requires you to sell the assets that have been increasing the most and buy more of the assets that have been declining the most. In other words, you buy low and sell high!

Another advantage gained by rebalancing is maintaining the risk level of the portfolio. Your diversified portfolio contains multiple assets, which provide different levels of expected return and risk. As the assets with higher expected returns in fact grow faster, it will concentrate a higher proportion of your portfolio in those assets, thereby increasing your level of risk. Automatic rebalancing removes this problem.

Another common tactic for those who are still working and regularly investing is using "dollar-cost averaging." Simply stated, dollar-cost averaging is investing the same dollar amount on a regular periodic basis, such as each pay period. By doing so, you will be purchasing fewer new shares when prices are high and more shares when they are low. This technique automatically produces a lower cost-per-share than purchasing at random times—especially when your instinct will be to purchase those investments that are gaining in market price! Caution! Dollar-cost averaging works against people who are withdrawing income from their portfolio rather than adding new money. See Chapter XIII—"Change to Income Investing."

Considering again the advantage of dividend-paying stocks over non-dividend-paying stocks, the automatic re-investment of dividends will provide additional leverage toward improving long-term growth by purchasing more shares when prices are low than when they are high.

The final piece is to work with a trusted advisor. He or she can help you design and implement an asset allocation portfolio that is consistent with your risk tolerance. Following implementation, this person's job is to keep you constant with your decision by discouraging any "tactical repositioning" of the portfolio.

Tactical moves are those repositioning moves motivated by your emotions telling you recent market, political, or financial happenings mean you need to adjust your strategy to either take advantage of or protect yourself from these external influences.

I know it is better to have a trusted outsider keeping you constant than it is to follow your feelings. I know this because it is easier for me to rationally advise a client than it is to resist these same emotions when it comes to my own investments. Think of yourself as a horse that's stable is on fire. If the horse is inside the burning structure, it can't be taken out without a blindfold, and if it's outside, instinct will tell it to go back in. The horse, like you, needs someone who can look at the situation more rationally.

But, you say, "People who were heavily in high tech stocks in 2000, 2001, and 2002 got killed." Yes, they did. However, the problem was created in 1997, 1998, and 1999 when emotions led these individuals to put more and more of their funds in higher-risk, poorly diversified portfolios. They were buying just because the price was increasing, as we discussed above.

But wouldn't it have been best for these individuals to get scared and sell early in the market decline? Yes, but evidence heavily suggests that the more you have become committed to a portfolio that is doing well, the harder it is to bail out early when the strategy fails. What most of these investors do in practice is ride their portfolio all, or most, of the way down. Once it is near the bottom, they sell out, book the losses, and wait until the market has somewhat recovered. This gives them a booked loss that will never be recaptured—irrespective of how well they may do with future investments. This explains the Dalbar Chart.

****

ANECDOTE

Art was a long-time client of our firm who "did his own thing" when it came to investing. He had done pretty well all through the 1990s. He planned to retire in 2001 when he turned 65, but was heavily over-weighted in high-tech stocks in his portfolio. The market broke in April 2000 and he lost half his portfolio value by the end of the year. However, he believed in these high-tech investments because they "had made me so much money"! He not only hung in there, he deferred his retirement, continued to work, and invested more in high-tech stocks to bring down his average cost-per-share. Unfortunately, the value of his portfolio dropped another 50 percent in 2001. He lost 75 percent of his portfolio value in less than 24 months—including all the new investments he had made in 2001. To raise money, Art sold his business, downsized his living expenses, and went to work in a firm on salary. In 2002, the value of his portfolio declined only a little—since he had liquidated most of his high-tech stocks and held the money in mostly fixed-income and cash. When the market (S&P 500) rebounded more than 30 percent in 2003, Art wasn't in the market and didn't recoup any of his prior losses.

****

NUGGET

Shares that have a price/earnings ratio of 50 or higher are not an investment, but rather, a speculation.

****

A trusted advisor can best keep you from getting a poorly diversified portfolio in the first place. An advisor can see to it that the portfolio has automatic rebalancing—so that if an asset class becomes "hot," you will be systematically selling and booking these profits, which can be invested in those asset classes, which are not hot. A trusted advisor can be your steadying influence when the broad market averages are in decline and the financial press is screaming that the end of the world is happening.

However, you might be retired and drawing regular monthly income from your invested assets. In other words, you are doing "reverse-dollar-cost averaging." For you, withdrawals when prices are low will require the sale of more shares and when they are high, it will require fewer shares be sold. See "Chapter XIV" on dealing with this problem.

Basically, this goes back to the selection of appropriate investments when you are living off the portfolio as compared to building it. One method is to hold investments that produce sufficient interest and dividends to provide the desired income without needing to liquidate shares. Another method is to liquidate shares for income only from asset classes that are not declining in value.

These investment selection issues as well as other considerations for retirees are covered in detail elsewhere in this book. As to the value of a trusted advisor in this later-in-life phase of managing your assets, for most people he or she will be both more and less important. He or she is more important because making a big mistake at this stage in life is impossible to offset. He or she is less important because your portfolio, once restructured, will most likely be more oriented toward fixed-income products and stocks that produce a stable cash flow, as compared to growth stocks. These investments are inherently more stable and require less oversight than those that you may have purchased to grow your portfolio. The advisor is there primarily to reassure you the portfolio is meeting your objectives and providing the desired income.

SUMMARY

- The average investor realizes returns dramatically below market returns, because investors chase the best-performing asset classes.
- Investors instinctively buy high and sell low.
- This issue can be addressed by diversification, automatic re-balancing, dollar cost averaging, and having an advisor to keep you with the program.
- The retiree should liquidate shares only from appreciated assets in order to meet income needs not covered by interest and dividends.

Chapter XII
SELECTING A FINANCIAL ADVISOR

Approximately 75 percent of people prefer to work with an investment advisor, stockbroker, insurance agent, mutual fund salesman, Chartered Financial Consultant or Certified Financial Planner. The first question is why.

With the advent of 401(K) plans and IRAs, this is coming into pretty good focus. The primary response people give in surveys is "they don't really understand enough about investing to be sure how to proceed." They hear terrible stories about people who have lost all or most of their money—so they feel more comfortable having a professional to help.

The balance of investors really want to develop their own investment and financial plans and only deal with professionals as transaction facilitators or occasionally as confirmation of the soundness of a concept or specific investment or investment approach. Whatever your approach, it is fine—as long as it truly is right for you. The thrust of this chapter is for the 75 percent of people who wish to deal with a Financial Advisor.

✳✳✳

ANECDOTE

Occasionally, I have had people in discussions that sound like a man I will call Charlie. Charlie was in my office discussing the concept of having him allow me to work with him as his investment advisor. Charlie had been referred to me by his CPA. I proposed putting together an investment program consistent with his risk tolerance using customized or standard asset allocation models through one of the investment management firms with which I place business. I proposed that my role as his investment advisor would be to help in putting him in the most appropriate asset allocation model, with the most suitable firm, then monitoring their performance to assure they were performing their job and meeting his objectives. In addition, my job would consist of periodic review with Charlie, helping him with managing his expectations, and living with the anxieties associated with investing. I would be paid for this work on a quarterly-fee basis, calculated as a percentage of the assets he placed through me.

As is our usual practice, Charlie and I completed our first meeting and scheduled a second meeting one week later—after he had an opportunity to consider what we had covered and read the material I sent with him.

At our second meeting, Charlie said, "I have reviewed all of this material and it sounds good, but I wonder why I can't just do the same thing myself without paying fees to you and the management company." I said, "You can certainly do that if you have the time to get and keep informed as well as the willingness to stay on top of it, and not be ruled by your emotions." He assured me he could, then proceeded to start asking questions pertinent to how to proceed. Needless to say, I politely informed him those were matters I cover with clients, but suggested that since he was doing it himself, he could find books at the library that might be helpful. He didn't seem to grasp why I was not more helpful.

❋❋

Fortunately, most people don't have Charlie's perspective. Most who want help appreciate that services cost money, but should result in a more satisfactory outcome if the advisor selected is competent and is a good fit for the individual. So, let's return to the question of how to select an advisor.

SIX STEPS TO FOLLOW

Much of selecting an advisor will be based upon feeling a comfort level with the individual selected. However, in getting there, you should do six things—even if you approached the potential advisor following a referral or already know him or her favorably from other activity:

1. Interview no less than three references who have done, or are doing, the same activity with the advisor that you are contemplating. These references should be enthusiastic about the advisor—especially if the reference's name was supplied by the advisor.

Beware the "Madoff factor"! In light of recent scandals such as Bernard Madoff, it is prudent to be careful when intrusting your money to someone. Like all professions, there are always some scoundrels about—though the great majority is honest and conscientious. Typically financial crooks will attempt to appeal to all three emotional weaknesses of investors—greed, fear, and the herd instinct. In addition, be very skeptical if he/she asks for "investment discretion" to manage your money—unless the actual funds are held and recorded by an outside "custodian." Ask for detail about his or her trading system—and don't invest unless you understand it.

It is best if the investment advisor has at least five years experience with the firm he or she currently represents. If he or she doesn't—or works as an independent—get a full picture of his or her professional background. Have any and all professional moves been improvements, lateral, setbacks? Confirm his or her answers to these questions as best you can.

2. Ask (don't be bashful) whether the advisor has any current or past disciplinary issues and, if so, what are the details? If they are prior issues that have been settled, ask for a copy of the finding. The advisor is required to answer these questions totally and honestly—or that is in itself a potential disciplinary issue. Before doing business with you, the advisor should voluntarily provide you with a government filing called a "Form ADV, Part II" that will provide you with this information.

3. Determine what education and training the potential advisor has acquired. Everyone will have "continuing education" requirements—so they are meaningless. What you are looking for is undergraduate or advanced degrees from accredited schools that indicate depth of learning in financial services. Examples of those degrees would include, but not be limited to, finance, insurance, investments or economics majors, Master of Science in Financial Services or other degrees that may be pertinent to the subject. What professional designation(s) is the person pursuing or already has? The three most common would be Chartered Financial Consultant (ChFC), Certified Financial Planner (CFP) and Chartered Life Underwriter (CLU). Whatever the designation(s), ask for details as to what and how a person obtains each designation, and the pedigree of the institution awarding it. The advisor should be enthusiastic about this information and give you a complete picture.

4. Is the advisor a company employee or independent? If the advisor is with a large firm, he or she will have company courses that can be very good—except company courses can provide a bias toward investments and/or insurance that fit the company's perspective of how things should

be done. For example, if the company only sells mutual funds, they will be unlikely to stress some of the advantages that may be found with variable or fixed annuities and vice versa if it is an insurance company that doesn't sell mutual funds. Companies logically stress those things they market and even if your potential advisor has the right to market nonproprietary investment and insurance products, he or she will be influenced toward the company view. Some investment companies even pay higher compensation for company-sponsored investments than those that are nonproprietary. (This practice has recently come under criticism, and may be illegal at the time you read this.) These factors can compromise objectivity. If you know about it, you can ensure that proprietary products are not the only things you are presented as investment and insurance choices and ask if the compensation is the same on either investment choice.

5. Can your prospective advisor handle both investments and insurance products? If he does only insurance, he can't do—and will be biased against—investment products. Vice versa if he only handles investments.

6. How will this advisor expect to be compensated? Ideally, the advisor is a "Registered Investment Advisor" (RIA) and will be compensated on a fee basis calculated as a percentage of assets under management. He may be a RIA in his own right or affiliated with a firm that is a RIA—either is fine.

Occasionally, you will find your advisor recommending an investment for which he will not be compensated on a fee basis. This is okay, but of course he should point it out and explain why. One example of this type of situation would be if an annuity is being recommended. Insurance companies usually compensate only by commissions. The advisor will get extra money now and reduced fees in the future since the "under management" amount will be reduced. To understand this, let's assume $200,000 is taken from an investment account to buy a single premium immediate annuity that will provide guaranteed life income. The advisor would typically be paid 3 percent ($6,000) one time and nothing in the future—though he retains minor future service obligations. He would lose future annual income ranging from about 1/4 percent to 1 percent on this $200,000 ($500-$2,000), which would be expected to increase in the years ahead as the amount under management grows. Another example could be if you are establishing an investment account of less than $100,000 for either yourself or a family member. In that situation, it may be better to buy a mutual fund that pays a commission. However, most mutual fund companies will pay a representative a 12b-1* commission quarterly (usually called "trail commissions" or "C shares"), rather than an upfront commission—depending upon the choice made by the advisor. You should insist upon the trail commissions as they total 1 percent per year based upon the assets in the fund and are therefore much like fees. For more about this, refer to the Chapter "Picking a Fund Company."

The reason you want your advisor compensated based upon assets under management whenever possible is to remove most conflicts of interest. You want his present and future compensation to be tied to the ongoing relationship and the success of the investments. If he gets all, or most, of his compensation upfront, the conflict is he only gets paid again if you buy something new. He becomes a salesman rather than an advisor with a long-term perspective.

****

NUGGETS

Advice from an "employee" of the product provider can't be presumed objective. EVEN IF NO ADDITIONAL COMPENSATION IS OFFERED TO PUSH THE PRODUCTS OF HIS OR HER EMPLOYER, THE PRESSURE TO SELL HIS COMPANY'S PRODUCTS IS ENOUGH THAT IT CAN HURT OBJECTIVITY.

If your broker/investment advisor never disagrees with you, what added value does he or she provide?—IS HE OR SHE JUST AN ORDER TAKER?

Brokers, agents, and financial advisors paid from trading costs have a conflict of interest with their client. THEIR INCENTIVES ARE TOWARD LOTS OF TRADING. YOURS SHOULD BE TOWARD LONG-TERM HOLDS.

Brokers, agents, and financial advisors paid commissions upfront have a conflict of interest with their client. THEIR INCENTIVES ARE TOWARD SWITCHING BETWEEN FUNDS. BUY AND HOLD USUALLY PRODUCES A BETTER RESULT.
****

* 12b-1 is the section of the federal code that provides for ongoing, fee like, compensation to brokers.

SUMMARY

• Find a good fit.

- Make sure the advisor has good supportive education and enough experience to be competent.
- The advisor should be open about how he does business and how he will be compensated.
- Determine any potential conflicts of interest and avoid or minimize them.
- He or she should have zero negative findings by regulatory authorities.
- His compensation should be competitive but not the cheapest; you are shopping for the best advisor, not the cheapest. Rarely will the best advisor also be the cheapest.

Chapter XIII
Long-Term Care Issues

Because Long-Term Care is so expensive and so common among seniors, "Investing for Income" must include a discussion of the increased income requirements attached to it.

GOVERNMENT BENEFITS ONLY FOR INDIGENT

Seniors, people sixty-five and over, generally center their sense of well being on maintaining their independence, both physical and financial. The connection that is too often not made is: Medicare payments for nursing home or "at-home" assisted-living expenses are restricted to highly skilled medical services (doctors and registered nurses), and increasingly more difficult to obtain. Dollar sums being paid out by Medicare in this category are actually declining. Since Medicare is already costing more than the taxes collected to fund it, the likelihood is this will get worse, not better. The greater expense though comes from "unskilled" services, which are not covered at all under Medicare.

Good planning requires that you proceed on the assumption that government benefits will not be available for long-term care unless you financially qualify for Medicaid. Medicaid is a program for the indigent. In other words, you become a ward of the state and give up your financial and physical independence. This "coverage" for long-term care is the situation people are concerned about when they worry about adequate financial resources in retirement.

Ninety-five percent of long-term care needs are "custodial" and therefore categorized as unskilled. Custodial Care is also sometimes called "assisted living." Patients require regular assistance in such things as bathing, dressing, transferring from bed to chair and back, toileting, and eating. These non-skilled services can be provided in an institutional setting or at home. At home, the services can be provided by paid professionals or a non-compensated member of the family. In other words, if you don't have the money for institutional or paid at-home assisted living, you will become a burden to either society or your family—exactly what the overwhelming percentage of seniors says they want to avoid.

A FAMILY BURDEN

In practice, 72 percent of people receiving long-term care services receive that service from a family member, at home. Twenty-five percent of informal family care-giving situations last five years or longer. This is consistent with long-term care industry statistics that show claims for community based long-term care last for 4–4.5 years.

Long-term care is primarily an issue for women. According to an AARP study (1999), 66 percent of custodial home care receivers are women, 70 percent of unpaid caregivers are women, and 75 percent of nursing home residents are women.

ARE YOU LIKELY TO NEED LONG-TERM CARE?

According to a 1998 National Home and Hospice Care Survey by Kris Hodges, at age sixty-five a person has a 72 percent chance of using home health care in their lifetime versus 49 percent likelihood of entering a nursing home.

Statistics indicate that those needing home or nursing home care will need those services for an average of five years or longer.

The move from home health care to a nursing home typically occurs when the home health care provider(s) are devoting sixty hours or more per week to care of the patient.

As life expectancies for the elderly continue to increase, the need for long-term care will increase. With each successive ten-year increment of age, the likelihood of being a current home care patient increases nearly two times.

THE COSTS ASSOCIATED WITH LONG-TERM CARE (LTC)

The cost of long-term care can be quite substantial. A recent Metropolitan Life Insurance Company survey of all fifty states determined that the average daily rate for nursing home care in 2004 was $181 for a private room and $153 for semiprivate. The average hourly rate for at home care by a Licensed Practical Nurse (LPN) was $37 and $18 for a Home Health Aid (HHA).

Based upon the above figures, the average for a semiprivate room in a nursing home exceeds $55,000 per year. The cost for an LPN for home health care for eight hours per day exceeds $108,000 and for an HHA exceeds $50,000. If you want a private room in a nursing home, it is more. If you need more than eight hours of home service, it is more. If you live in an expensive state such as California, New York, or Hawaii, it is more. If you can't afford to pay for it, the cost is often paid by having a family member give up paid employment to provide the care. It is oftentimes paid for by invading college funds for grandchildren or retirement funds of children.

Given that these costs are in addition to regular living expenses, the effect on the senior or senior couple's financial well being can be devastating. So, are there ways this money can be provided without bankrupting the senior, the couple, or their children?

PAY FROM SAVINGS

If you have an extra $250,000 to $1,000,000 that could be used to provide you and your spouse with long-term care if needed, you can probably relax. With these funds conservatively invested so it will grow as long-term care costs grow, you can probably meet any long-term care needs without changing your living standard or asking the kids for help.

BUY OR LEASE INTO A PLANNED-TOTAL SERVICES RETIREMENT COMMUNITY

There are many planned retirement communities that include both Assisted Living and Nursing Home Care in addition to standard apartments or cottages. This industry is now more than thirty-five years old—so the issues that usually have to be resolved when a new concept is launched have pretty well been worked out.

There are both for-profit and nonprofit offerings. There are both buying with a life estate (ownership until you die) and leased services. I am not recommending one of these facilities, necessarily, but have had very successful personal experience with one facility. This experience was through my parents. They purchased a life estate in a community with a very nice apartment, plus garage and typical senior living amenities for healthy people. Their purchase also made them eligible for both Assisted Living and Nursing Home care on the premises, as needed. My father used the nursing home facility, and my mother used both the nursing home and assisted living.

Those facilities where you buy-in with a life estate in the facility are usually nonprofit and have lower monthly fees—reflecting the fact capital is provided by the residents rather than outside investors. Lease facilities are more likely to be for-profit and have higher monthly fees that reflect the required return on capital for the investors. I have been told some well-established facilities now have an option to lease for one year as a trial period. At the end of the year, you must either buy-in or move.

Which type, buy-in or lease, is better depends on the customer's preferences and available capital. If you are going to investigate this method of retirement living, you should look at two or three facilities of each type—rather than taking the first that makes a fine sounding presentation. Part of this should, of course, include talking off the record with residents while on the premises. Obviously, extensive due diligence of the financial condition of the facility is a most important factor in making a final decision.

LIFE INSURANCE POLICY

For details, see Chapter VI on "Retirement Uses for Life Insurance." Briefly, life insurance is originally purchased to benefit your survivors after your death. When LTC occurs, life insurance can often be used to benefit the patient—as well as those who may otherwise face the burden of care—through accelerated death benefits and negotiated settlements. A situation in which the care recipient can retain his or her own financial and personal independence is certainly a living benefit to all.

REVERSE MORTGAGE ON YOUR RESIDENCE

If you and your spouse are both age sixty-two or older, the equity in your home may be a ready source of tax-free funds to pay LTC expenses. Rather than refinancing with a conventional mortgage, which will require monthly payments, a better way may be to take out a "reverse mortgage" on your primary residence.

A reverse mortgage is a non-recourse loan against equity in your home that may provide either monthly income, an account to tap for expenses, or both. The funds received are not taxable and the lender cannot foreclose on the loan as long as at least one of the mortgagees remains living there and proper maintenance and insurance are provided.

There is no need to qualify with good credit since you are not taking on an obligation to pay back the loan. The guarantor of the loan is the property itself and your equity in it. You could be in a shaky financial position (possibly due to past LTC expenses), take out a reverse mortgage, pay off those bills, and have some left for future expenses. You may have an existing conventional mortgage on the property. Use a reverse mortgage to pay off that loan and decrease your monthly expenses so you can pay LTC costs.

If you have, or are planning to buy, long-term care insurance, the availability of a reverse mortgage, if needed, can permit you to take as long as possible a waiting period before benefits begin in order to keep premiums as low as possible.

Some seniors have an emotional block to considering a reverse mortgage. They have sacrificed to pay for their home and, at first blush, it feels to them as though they are putting it back at risk. Though understandable, on further reflection it is clear it actually makes the property foreclosure-proof and therefore more secure. Especially at a time when potentially onerous expenses are being accumulated, this may be the safest way to meet them.

Others have said to me, "But I was planning for the house to be what I left for the kids!" Again, this is understandable. We all develop long-term goals that are hard to put aside. Another way to think about this objective might be to use that equity to benefit them now through freedom from providing care or financial support. Not only that, isn't your objective to remain in your home, remain financially independent, and remain physically independent? If a reverse mortgage can be a major tool to help make that happen, it is probable both you and the kids will be happier with that than an inheritance after your death.

LONG-TERM CARE INSURANCE

From a slow start, LTC Insurance has evolved to effective, flexible coverage at competitive rates. Because of the slow start, many people incorrectly have the impression that the cost/benefit of this type policy is not good.

That used to be true! However, now that the actuaries have sufficient experience to price the product accurately and with many competitors seeking your business, you can find quality offerings at a reasonable price.

For two reasons you should acquire LTC insurance as young as you can. One is because LTC coverage is medically underwritten. The other is because the price dramatically increases with age. As a rule of thumb, the premium about doubles with each decade you wait to begin coverage.

As to medical qualifications, it is neither like qualifying for life insurance nor qualifying for health insurance. For example, severe arthritis will probably not disqualify you for either life or health insurance, but it may be a problem for LTC insurance if it affects your ability to dress yourself or perform other daily life functions. As an example, coronary artery disease could be a problem for life and health insurance, but may not cause a problem in qualifying for LTC insurance.

Factors other than age and health affecting the cost of LTC coverage are:

- Length of the waiting period from commencement of the problem until the time the insurance will begin paying benefits;
- Daily benefit the insurance will pay for various services;
- Length of time the benefits will be paid.

Chapter XIV
CHANGE TO INCOME INVESTING

During the accumulation of your retirement savings, you will have become familiar and comfortable with investment industry terms such as total return, growth potential, price volatility, buying opportunity, market momentum, and patience. During retirement, when your current and future standard of living may be based upon the ability of your investments to produce a dependable stream of inflation-adjusted income, the above concepts have little practical value.

Your new favorite terms are consistent and growing dividend history, rock-solid financial statements, consistent performance, predictability, assured, and guaranteed.

Reaching retirement age requires a complete change of perspective about investing if you are to not outlive your investment assets. Before retirement, your objective was "growth in the value of your portfolio and increasing the number of shares you own." After retirement, the objective is "meeting your income requirements for as long as you, or you and your spouse, live."

This does not mean you should never invest in the stock market. As a matter of fact, it is all but impossible for most retirees to sustain an adequate and growing income stream without some equities. The issue is how much should be in equities and what type.

STOCKS TO HOLD IN RETIREMENT

Many seniors own few, if any, stocks. Many seniors who hold stocks have inappropriate holdings for their situation. Though it is not appropriate to tell any individual through these pages what to buy or hold, there are certain types and classes of stocks that are generally more suitable for seniors. When referring to stocks, I include stock mutual funds and exchange traded funds (ETFs).

ISSUES FOR HOLDING STOCKS

Seniors (sixty-five and over) generally have three basic issues as they relate to the ownership of stocks.

- The issue of price stability.
- The issue of dependable income.
- The issue of inflation protection.

Volatility, (lack of price stability) is the issue that keeps many, if not most, seniors out of the stock market. As the realization that you need stability and predictability in your finances becomes apparent, it is too easy to conclude there is no place for stocks in your investments. Many of us have experienced, or seen firsthand, the devastation a major drop in the market can produce. If that is your general position, let me have you consider this—not all stocks are created equal!

The calendar years 2000, 2001, and 2002 gave us the largest decline in the overall stock market since the great depression (The bear market of 2008 has not run its course as of this writing.) However, that decline was not distributed evenly across the entire market. The worst hit was taken by so-called "high-tech" stocks. Conversely, real estate stocks (REITs) experienced a major increase in price.

Why the difference? High-tech stocks generally have little or no earnings, pay small or no dividends if they have earnings, but are perceived to represent companies that are the big, profitable firms of tomorrow. People who buy these stocks are speculating upon the value of the earnings and dividends in the future, and making a bet. Conversely, most REITs are purchased for their current income and the potential inflation protection provided by anticipated rent increases in the future. Growth stocks, like high-tech stocks, are generally not an appropriate retirement income investment. Income-producing stocks, like real estate investment trusts, are generally an appropriate retirement income investment.

High-tech stocks drove the market bubble in the late '90s. REITs were undervalued by the market at that time because the income of 10 percent to 15 percent looked skimpy compared to the 25 percent to 50 percent appreciation being posted by growth stocks, led by High Tech. These two extremes make the point that owning stocks for stability is not the point as much as what kind of stocks. Had you purchased REITs in the late nineties you would have purchased an income stream substantially higher than bonds. If you buy REITs today REITs will still pay dividends higher than bonds. As I write this (February 2009)) REIT prices are declining as part of the 2008-2009 bear market and the dividend to price ratio is moving up. In other words, REITs are valued more like a bond than a stock in that pricing and yield move in opposite directions. They could be a bond substitute for part of your portfolio.

As a matter of fact, all stocks and funds that pay dividends possess this attribute to some degree in that dividends are not as volatile as market price. "Many issues which experience a drop in market price will not experience a drop in the dividend." We discussed this in more detail in Chapter VII and below in this Chapter.

CONVERTIBLES

"Preferred Convertible Stock" is another type of stock that has characteristics much different from those growth stocks, which get all the investment press. Simply, these stocks have both stock and bond characteristics. A corporation may choose to issue preferred stock rather than bonds because it can do so with lower dividend expense than would be the interest on issuing bonds. The stock receives a "preferred dividend" which may be competitive with bond yields of the same company if compared to the after tax yield to the investor, but at more risk to the investor as the claim of debt owners is superior to the claim of all stockholders. Offsetting that higher risk compared to bonds is the fact that preferred convertible stock may, under certain circumstances, be convertible to common stock so the investor can partially share in the growth potential of the company. In addition, the risk to the investor before conversion is less than common stock as both the dividend and the liquidation value have preference over common shares.

STOCKS PAYING DIVIDENDS
(Usually value, as opposed to growth, stocks)

Dividend-paying stocks are generally stocks of older, better-established companies who usually set a dividend payout rate from their relatively predictable profits. They work extra hard to hold that payout rate once established. With the advent of more favorable tax treatment of dividends, more corporations that are in a position to do so are establishing what they intend to be a relatively predictable annual dividend. (For additional information, see Chapter VII.)

The dividends (other than for REITs) tend to be low relative to debt securities during normal markets, generally in the range of 1–3 percent of the underlying market value of the shares. However, as the value of the underlying stock appreciates over time, the dividend will also tend to grow. This can mean that the dividend yield of a successful company's shares could, over time, produce more income than the yield from the same company's bonds.

Owning some of these stocks, or a mutual fund or exchange-traded fund of them will provide a relatively stable cash flow plus the opportunity for income appreciation over time.

"REVERSE" DOLLAR COST AVERAGING

During the accumulation of your retirement fund, you may have made use of dollar cost averaging. This is a technique whereby you hold down the average cost per share in your portfolio by purchasing an equal dollar amount of stocks and bonds on a periodic basis. This automatically buys more shares when prices are down and fewer shares when prices are up. Of course the same applies to the purchase of shares of a stock or bond fund, too.

As a retiree who needs to withdraw periodic payments for living expenses, you trigger a reverse of dollar cost averaging if you are selling shares to provide income. As prices go up, you liquidate fewer shares and as prices decline, you will liquidate more shares. This makes a declining market doubly painful to the person drawing income if required to sell shares. This again speaks to the need to hold dividend-paying stocks in retirement rather than growth stocks, which generally do not pay dividends.

PORTFOLIO FAILURE

Modern Portfolio Theory helps the investor handle risk by concentrating on the market value fluctuations of various diversified portfolios rather than stock picking or market timing. Risk is defined as "the amount of anticipated price volatility." (See Chapter VIII on Indexing.) The investor then only needs to select the portfolio with the risk tolerance he or she believes she can live with in both good and bad markets.

The retiree drawing income has the additional risk of portfolio failure! The possibility that the withdrawal rate of income could draw down the portfolio to the point it can no longer make the withdrawal payments.

From the standpoint of risk of portfolio failure the "Bengen Study" (1994) provides some valuable guidance as to how much a person drawing income should have in equities and how much in fixed-income.

The study covers the fifty-year period from 1926–1976. This is an ideal period for the study because it covers three wars, the Great Depression, and the hyperinflation of the 1970s—as well as the good times during the 1920s, 1950s and 1960s.

It is not my purpose here to outline the entire study, but rather to give you his insights that have been validated and accepted by the academic community. The conclusions are (paraphrased):

- A "4 percent withdrawal rate" is optimum and used for the other conclusions.
- Retirement portfolios for those drawing income should have no less than a 50 percent stock (equity) allocation and no more than a 75 percent stock allocation.
- The only positive feature of stock allocation above 50 percent is that the ending values grow substantially more for those portfolios that do not fail.
- Portfolios that had 25 percent or less allocated to stocks had substantially higher risk of portfolio failure than portfolios with 50 percent or more allocated to stocks.

Warning! This is wonderful information, but it is only a guide or starting point. Your retirement years will be different to some degree from the years covered in the study.

Your needs relative to your means may differ as the study assumes the need and desire to maximize income at very low risk of portfolio failure. If, as an example, you have substantial annuity style income that covers all basic expenses as well as most of recreation and travel, you may not need to draw as much as 4 percent of the investment portfolio.

The Bengen study, discussed above, and all other studies not covered here, don't account for the flexibility of retirees to adjust income when required or the tendency of retirees to require less income as they age.

WITHDRAWAL STRATEGIES

There are three basic strategies, with almost unlimited variations stemming from those three:

- FLAT ANNUITY. In this strategy, cash withdrawals are set at a dollar amount per month, per quarter, or per year with the objective of continuing this amount each period until the annuitant dies.
- INFLATION-ADJUSTED ANNUITY. With this strategy, the objective is to have the annuity income adjust periodically (usually annually) to keep the purchasing power constant until the annuitant dies.
- PERFORMANCE-BASED ANNUITY. This strategy calls for linking the payment amount of the annuity to the earnings of an investment portfolio.

The insurance industry provides both flat annuities and performance-based annuities. The industry jargon calls these "Fixed Annuities" and "Variable Annuities." In either case, they provide an income stream for life. For further details, see Chapter V "Annuities."

Inflation-adjusted annuities are not as readily available. Since the inflation rate is unpredictable, pricing this product would be very difficult. In periods of high inflation, such as the 1970s, you could do great financial harm to the insurance company. During periods of low inflation such as the 1980s and 1990s, the annuitant would be getting a significantly lower return per dollar invested than he would have had with a Fixed Annuity.

A practical method many people use to address this problem is to divide their annuity income between a fixed and a variable annuity, often 50/50. Fixed to provide the dollar floor and the variable to protect against inflation through its investment in an equity portfolio. This is not a perfect solution, but one that may enhance long-term satisfaction for that portion of your portfolio that is committed to annuities.

WITHDRAWAL METHODS

THE LIFE ANNUITY METHOD is built around the concept of buying a "life annuity" to provide income equivalent to 3–5 percent of your total portfolio before the annuity purchase.

The portion of the portfolio, which is not used to purchase the life annuity, will stay invested as a side fund to provide additional funding as necessary to offset an increasing need for income caused by inflation or other factors. If this side fund accumulation can be done through a tax-favored account such as an IRA or a "deferred" annuity, so much the better.

When or if the time arrives when it is desirable to increase the monthly life income amount, funds can be used from the side fund to buy more annuity income. Of course, if the side fund is already in a deferred annuity, all you need to do is annuitize a portion.

This method helps solve the need for an "inflation-adjusted annuity" without excessive risk to the insurer or too expensive premiums for the annuitant.

THE PERIOD CERTAIN ANNUITY METHOD is designed to obtain the benefits of the set monthly income without the features of a "Life Annuity." With the period certain annuity, you need not use a life insurance company if you find a better alternative as there is no assumption of a mortality risk by the annuity issuer.

With a period certain annuity, you would buy a set monthly income for a set number of months or years rather than life. This will require liquidating a smaller percentage of your portfolio to buy the annuity payments. For example, a life annuity of $1,000 per month for a male age sixty-five may cost $153,900 whereas a ten-year period certain annuity for the same person for $1,000 per month may cost $94,281— (61 percent less).

Retirees may choose the period certain annuity approach rather than the life annuity approach for several reasons, including:

Health of the prospective annuitant(s) may be poor leading to an expectancy of living too short a time to benefit from the lifetime feature of the life annuity.

The objective may be to fill in an income gap such as years remaining until Social Security begins.

A desire to have the income stability but retain more of the investment upside over time to enhance later income or maximize the portfolio at death for the estate's beneficiaries.

THE FIVE-YEAR SAFETY STOCK PLAN

This plan is designed for the retiree who wishes to withdraw monthly income from his/her portfolio while wishing to retain the principal as much as possible.

To illustrate the plan, we will assume our retiree has a $1,000,000 portfolio and wishes to withdraw 5 percent ($50,000) each year. We have him put $500,000 in a fixed-income portfolio, and $500,000 in an equity portfolio.

The first year, he will spend $50,000 from the fixed-income portfolio. At the end of year one, he will sell $50,000 of stock to replenish the fixed-income portfolio to $500,000, but "only if the stock has appreciated sufficiently" to do so. If the equities have appreciated less than $50,000 (10.0 percent), or even declined in value, he will limit equity sales to the amount to bring the equity account back down to $500,000. In other words, "his withdrawals will be taken from the fixed-income portfolio except to the extent they can be covered by appreciation and dividends in the equity portfolio."

This procedure restricts liquidation of equity shares to the amount that can be covered by appreciation and dividends. It is possible that down markets in equities could last five or six years and severely reduce the fixed-income portfolio through withdrawals. This is highly improbable as down markets last an average of eighteen months. In addition, we said replenish $50,000 when in actuality the $450,000 of debt securities not consumed in year one will have earned from 2–5 percent or $9,000 to $22,500. In year two, $400,000 produces $8,000 to $20,000 and so on. From a practical standpoint, you could probably run seven or eight years withdrawing only from the fixed-income side before the portfolio was getting so unbalanced from the 50/50 mix that the risk factors are becoming excessively different.

It is important to maximize the return of the fixed-income portion of the plan. If you put it all in a money market account, or other cash equivalent, the low yield will be a risk factor for the possibility of portfolio failure. During most periods, it is better to buy a combination of money market for the current year and laddered bonds, CDs and other fixed-income securities for the next four years and beyond.

In year one, we spend the funds from the money market account—ensuring that we don't spend more than our target of 3–5 percent of the entire portfolio value at the beginning of the year. This should leave a little cash from the interest earnings on the first anniversary. Additionally, we will have from $9,000–22,500 of interest from the $450,000 of bonds. For discussion, assume the interest income totals $20,000. We therefore need to replenish $30,000 at the end of year one that has been depleted from the fixed-income account.

But wait! If we have concentrated our equity investing in REITs, Preferred Stock, and other dividend-paying stocks, we may have realized from $10,000–20,000 or more of income. This can replenish the fixed-income allocation before any necessity to sell shares. Assuming we received $15,000 from our equity income, we now have only a $15,000 reduction in our fixed-income portion of the portfolio—though we have withdrawn $50,000.

We then look to the growth in the equity account. If the equity account has grown by $15,000 (3 percent) or more, you sell enough of the appreciation to bring back the fixed-income side to a full 50 percent of your investment portfolio. For example, let us say the appreciation on the equity $500,000 was 10 percent or $50,000. Your account now looks like:

ILLUSTRATION I

Fixed account value at start of year =	**$500,000**
Withdrawal for living expenses	**<$50,000>**
Interest plus Dividends	**$35,000**
Total end of year =	**$485,000**
Equity account value at start of year =	**$500,000**
Appreciation	**$50,000**
Total end of year =	**$550,000**
Total Year end portfolio value =	**$1,035,000**

To rebalance our portfolio to 50 percent fixed-income and 50 percent equity, we need to sell $32,500 of the equity appreciation and put it in fixed-income. At the beginning of year two, we will then have $517,500 in the equity account (50 percent) and $517,500 (50 percent) in the fixed-income account.

The fixed-income account at the beginning of year two will be comprised of:

$50,000 one-year bonds maturing and going to the money market account for year two distributions.
$50,000 two-year bonds with one year remaining to maturity.
$50,000 three-year bonds with two years remaining to maturity.
$50,000 four-year bonds with three years remaining to maturity.
$67,500 new four-year bonds purchased from liquidated equity securities plus non-distributed interest and dividends. $32,500 plus $35,000 = $67,500
$250,000 other fixed-income securities
$517,500 total fixed-income investment at start of second year

A "PERFORMANCE-BASED" FIVE-YEAR SAFETY STOCK PLAN

Using our results above for performance based distributions would mean we would increase the 5 percent/$50,000 distribution to 5 percent of $1,035,000 = $51,750. We would reduce the new four-year bond purchase by $1,750 and deposit the cash in the money market account for distribution.

FIVE-YEAR SAFETY STOCK PLAN WHEN THE MARKET DECLINES

Using our numbers above, with the only change being that our equity portfolio declines 10 percent rather than appreciates 10 percent, gives the following result at the end of year one.

Our fixed-income portfolio has been reduced by a net $15,000 from withdrawals to $485,000 as in the illustration above.

Our equity portfolio has declined in value by $50,000 to $450,000.

This gives us a total portfolio of $935,000 to fund year two. A decline in our nest egg of $65,000 (-6.5 percent).

We set aside $50,000 from the fixed-income side in a money market account for year-two spending, which leaves $435,000 in fixed-income securities and $450,000 in equities. The $885,000 portfolio is 50.85 percent in equities and 49.15 percent in fixed-income at the start of year two. Remember, we don't sell equities to get back to 50/50 unless we are selling equity growth for the year in question.

In year two, we can expect about $30,975 of dividend and interest income. Let us assume an additional reduction of 5 percent in the market value of the equity portfolio. At the end of year two, our portfolio has been reduced by a net $19,025 from withdrawals to $465,975 and equities have lost 5 percent or $22,500.

ILLUSTRATION II (end of year two)
Our fixed-income portfolio

Miscellaneous Fixed-income Securities	$250,000
Remaining in Money Market	$65,975
Laddered Bonds or CDs	$150,000
TOTAL Fixed-income portfolio	$465,975
Beginning Equity Portfolio value	$450,000
Unrealized Loss of 5 percent	<$22,500>
TOTAL Equity Portfolio	$427,500

TOTAL portfolio value end of year 2   **$893,475**

Even though there was a loss of 5 percent in the equity portfolio, it remains at 47.85 percent of the total—but reduced—portfolio. In two years, our total portfolio has declined 10.65 percent, but we have not sold any equity securities at a loss or liquidated fixed-income securities at less than par.

When the third year unfolds, we will receive about $31,000 in interest from the fixed-income and stock dividend income plus the equity portfolio gains 15 percent for our example. At the end of year three, our portfolio would be:

ILLUSTRATION III
TOTAL Fixed-income portfolio end of year 3   <u>**$446,975**</u>

Beginning Equity Portfolio value   **$427,500**
Unrealized appreciation of 15 percent   <u>**$64,125**</u>
TOTAL Equity Portfolio end of year 3   <u>**$491,625**</u>

TOTAL portfolio value end of year 3   **$938,600**

During the three-year period, our portfolio has become out of balance. 52.38 percent is in equity and 47.62 percent in fixed-income. However, this is a five-year program. The theory is that the equity portfolio will appreciate enough to rebalance to 50/50 percent by selling only equity growth above $500,000 before we run out of the five-year period. If that is not the case at the end of five years, you should probably rebalance to 50/50 percent anyway, if that is your comfortable allocation.

A PERFORMANCE-BASED FIVE-YEAR STOCK SAFETY PLAN

This plan would reduce income starting with year two in our illustration. For example, year two distributions would be only $46,750 at 5 percent because the portfolio had declined in value to $935,000. This is a reduction of $3,250, or about $271 per month. This will result in the portfolio declining less rapidly and therefore returning to the starting value with less equity growth.

Obviously, the five-year safety stock plan, which is not performance adjusted, has a bigger risk (though marginally) of portfolio failure.

The performance-based five-year SSP is safer, but requires living with varying income levels, which many seniors find uncomfortable.

To smooth out, somewhat, the variability of income, some retirees base the withdrawal amount on a percentage of the last three years' account values, rather than the immediate past year only. This smoothing of the base number smoothes the speed at which the income declines in a bear market and increases in a bull market, thereby reducing the instability of income.

PERCENTAGES ABOVE 50 PERCENT IN EQUITIES

It may be desirable to have more than 50 percent in equities of the type that pay dividend income.

FIRST: Bengen says the only advantage of having more than 50 percent in equities is the value of the portfolio in the estate. However, if you concentrate equities in REITs and other dividend stocks up to 75 percent of the portfolio, another advantage could be you may not need to rely on appreciation to cover the income shortfall, as there may be none.

SECOND: Dividends on dividend-paying stocks, including REITs, are often more stable and predictable than interest rates on fixed-income securities. This appears to be so because interest rates are the result of Federal Reserve action and ups and downs of market-generated yields as the economy goes through its various cycles. In contrast, the dividend yield of a stock is usually pegged by management as a conservative portion of their earnings trend line that they intend to maintain through both bull and bear markets. Failure to maintain an established dividend payout per share will be read by the market that management is underperforming, and thereby further depress the market price of their stock.

Therefore, in my own retirement portfolio, I have not hesitated to be more than 50 percent in dividend-paying equities to reduce or eliminate the need to be dependent on the appreciation of assets to meet my income needs.

WITHDRAWAL SEQUENCE:

Sequencing taxable and tax-favored accounts or annuities can make a difference in the after-tax benefits you can spend in retirement. The general rule is to spend taxable accounts down to zero prior to taking voluntary amounts from your tax-deferred accounts.

This generally is better since payments from the taxable accounts will have a cost basis. This can make a portion of each distribution tax-free until basis is recovered in those situation where principal is part of the payment. It is further advantageous as it allows your tax-deferred accounts to continue to grow in both value and number of shares without the taxman diluting the growth.

For tax-deferred accounts where the contributions were also tax deductible (such as an IRA), Required Minimum Distributions (RMD) will have to be taken starting in the year in which you turn 70.5 years. The custodian of these accounts, or your financial planning advisor, can guide you through the many options available in determining how these minimum distributions are calculated.

SPECIAL TAXABLE ACCOUNT CONSIDERATIONS

If the portfolio from which you are drawing income is a taxable—or mostly taxable—account, there are special tax-planning considerations. You would still split the portfolio about 50/50, or more, between stocks and bonds or annuities and take your distributions from the fixed-income side. What is special is the desire to draw income from the place with the smallest tax penalty—while still following the rules of a well run withdrawal plan such as those discussed above.

The interest from tax-free municipal bonds may be appropriate for the fixed-income side if they yield enough and don't conflict with Social Security and Medicare benefits. The interest income from annuities and bonds or CDs is federally taxed at your highest marginal tax rate (a maximum of 35 percent currently). Stock appreciation and stock dividends—other than dividends from REITs, which are taxed at ordinary rates—are taxed at the federal level at a maximum of 15 percent under current law.

Therefore, in drawing income from the portfolio you want to:

- See if the income from tax-free municipal bonds can meet all or some of your income needs.
- Take the stock dividends as income rather than letting them be automatically reinvested. Of course, excess income should be reinvested.

- Systematically liquidate a combination of principal plus interest from fixed-income in order to recapture basis and hold down your tax bill. This can be done personally with a calculation each year as illustrated above, or buy the principal and interest distributions from an investment company, bank, or insurance company.
- Replenish the fixed-income side by liquidating appreciation on the stock side that will be taxed at a maximum 15 percent under current capital gains law. Pay the tax and that money now has basis that can be recaptured at the ordinary income rate as you liquidate principal.
- If you wish to consider using an annuity for some portion of the income from this taxable portfolio, you may want to consider purchase of a "gift annuity" from a charitable institution that you would like to favor with a gift. Purchase of this gift annuity from taxable funds will provide tax benefits up front as well as during the withdrawal period.

We mentioned at the top of this chapter that income investing requires that you look at your portfolio differently than you did while you were building it. Systematically liquidating principal is one reason requiring that change in mindset. You have to realize that when drawing a set amount monthly to live on, you are always drawing out an amount that would have added to principal if you were building the portfolio. Therefore, if you withdraw only income from interest or REIT dividends, you will pay your top marginal ordinary rate. If you withdraw interest and principal, you will only pay ordinary income tax on the portion attributable to interest. If you receive income from regular dividends and liquidate only appreciation from your stocks, you will pay the lower rate for capital gains and dividends.

One of the simple ways to accomplish the above besides taking stock dividends in cash is to purchase a "period-certain annuity" for a period certain of ten years or so.

You should consult with your CPA or financial planner about these tax issues since congress has a propensity to make periodic changes that could change how you would address the above issues.

WHICH METHOD, LIFE ANNUITY, PERIOD CERTAIN ANNUITY, VARIABLE ANNUITY, FIVE-YEAR SAFETY STOCK PLAN, PERFORMANCE FIVE-YEAR SSP, OR A COMBINATION OF SEVERAL METHODS, IS BEST FOR YOU?

That will depend upon personal circumstances, willingness to live with uncertainty, margins available to fund retirement, and estate-planning objectives. However, a few general statements can be made.

- Annuity solutions will tend to be more popular with those who have little or no experience in managing a portfolio.
- Annuity solutions will tend to be more popular with those retirees who do not wish to burden themselves with periodic review meetings and decision-making.
- The initial decision whether or not to be intimately involved in the retirement investment management decisions may change as age, health changes, and deaths occur to a retiree or retirement couple.
- Your decision on these issues may be strongly influenced by whether or not you have a trusted advisor who can assist you in these decisions and calculations.

CHAPTER XV
PUTTING YOUR PLAN
TOGETHER

Now that you have spent a fair amount of time reading about investing your money for income, the question arises "How do I put this all together in a coherent plan?".

There are three basic steps:

1. Determine the amount of need for income during retirement.
2. Measure the ability of your current portfolio to do the job.
3. Use your newly acquired knowledge to fine-tune your plan.

DETERMINE THE NEED

The first chore is to determine the income you will need to maintain your current lifestyle for the entire period of you and your spouse's lifetimes. Almost any bookstore will have a book on budgeting. However, for our purposes, let's just assume you will need and want 100 percent of your pre-retirement income. Use a "budget guide" that will help you determine that amount, the resources available to meet it, and the amount to which you will be dependent upon your investment assets to succeed.

If your plan is to work with a financial planner or advisor, I suggest you complete a budget before your first meeting. It will help him or her to quickly see your financial situation as it applies to retirement income needs. Also, have the advisor read this book before your first meeting. This could give you both a good starting point for your discussion and planning.

It is true that retirees often find their cash-income requirements are reduced in order to remain in their current situation. Reasons often include savings from not paying Social Security taxes; a primary residence that is paid for; moving to a retirement community where costs are lower; no need to save aggressively for retirement; relief from required costs of working; etc. Many so-called "authorities" assert you can "stay in your own world" on 70 percent to 80 percent of your pre-retirement income. However, everyone's planning contains responsibilities and benefits unique to their situation. Best to shoot for 100 percent and turn to those areas that may afford savings if your income requires something less.

IS THE NEED COVERED?

The second and more difficult chore is to determine whether your assets and benefits structure will cover your need. Fortunately, there are software programs that can help with this process. My favorite is a program called "Planningworx." At this time, I don't know if you can acquire it at retail, but many Investment and Financial Advisors subscribe to their service and will use it in helping you put together a comprehensive plan. For a complete search of planning tools available, Google "retirement software."

Planningworx asks fifteen basic questions from which the software will run three tests to determine if your sources of income meet your objectives. These questions are:

- Your name?
- Your age?
- What year do you plan to retire?
- What is your monthly pension when you retire?
- What Cost of Living (COLA) will this pension income receive?
- What monthly gross income do you want to receive when you retire?
- What inflation rate should we assume for this income?
- What is the current value of assets that may be devoted to providing this income?
- How much will you save yearly until retirement?
- What is the estimated average return you will receive until you retire?
- What is the estimated average return you will receive after you retire?

- In what year will your additional monthly retirement income begin (spouse pension and/or Social Security)?
- What is the monthly amount you expect from Social Security?
- What COLA adjustment will this income receive?
- What will be your investment asset allocation?

Regardless of which, if any, planning software or financial advisor you use, keeping these basic questions in front of you will help you assure the basic facts are being covered.

APPLY WHAT YOU HAVE LEARNED

- No investment or savings choices are without risk.
- Setting realistic investment expectations and avoiding greed, fear, and the herd instinct are essential to investment success.
- Income tax planning can pay big dividends if risk is not increased to accomplish it.
- Fixed-income assets that are default risk free will usually not meet return objectives and will usually result in a loss of purchasing power over time.
- Annuities are a useful income-planning tool for retirees.
- Paid-up life insurance can be an excellent retirement asset.
- Income from stock and REIT dividends is much more stable than the market price of the underlying securities.
- Dividend-paying stocks are superior to growth stocks over time.
- Choosing indexing or active management of your investments can have a significant impact on your outcome.
- Real Estate Investment Trusts are superior retirement income investments.
- Not all fund companies are equal.
- Having a trusted advisor can be worth more than his or her fees.
- Not all advisors are created equal.
- Long-Term Care expenses are a probable expense of retirement.
- Income investing is different from accumulation investing and has the added risk of portfolio failure.

This is not the end, but the end of the beginning of your retirement income project! Good luck!

About the Author

Curtis R. (Curt) Bryant has spent his entire adult life in the financial services industry beginning in 1954, part time, when he was a college student.

During this more than half-century of experience, he has worked as a life insurance agent, securities registered representative, and as both a field and home office manager.

In 1986, Curt and his wife Pat founded their own Pension Consulting firm in Southern California. The firm specialized in administration and investment management of qualified plans for both small commercial companies and professional firms. This firm was sold to Assurity Advisors, Inc. (formerly Pine Lake Advisors, Inc.) in December 2005. Pat continues to provide some consulting services for this National Pension services firm. Curt retired December 31, 2008.

Curt and Pat are authors of "The Pension Primer / Retirement Plan Handbook" published in 1993.

Curt took his undergraduate studies at DePauw University in Greencastle, Indiana, and later received a Master's Degree in Financial Services from The American College in Bryn Mawr, Pennsylvania.

Professionally, he holds the designations, Chartered Life Underwriter (CLU), Chartered Financial Consultant (ChFC), and Certified Senior Advisor (CSA).

Suggested Reading List

"PREPARING FOR RETIREMENT" Financial security in uncertain times. Larry Burkett, Moody Press, Chicago, 1992, ISBN: 0-8024–6383-5

"THE NEW RETIREMENT" How to secure financial freedom and live out your dreams. Dan Benson, Word Publishing, Nashville, 2000, ISBN: 0-8499-4248-9

"FINANCIAL DECISIONS FOR RETIREMENT" David A. Littell & Kenn Beam Tacchino, The American College Press, Bryn Mawr, PA 2005, ISBN: 1932819177

"STOCKS FOR THE LONG RUN" A Guide to Selecting Markets for Long Term Growth, Jeremy J. Siegel, Irwin Professional Publishing, Chicago, 1994, ISBN: 1-55623-804-5

"THE FUTURE FOR INVESTORS" Why the Tried and the True Triumph Over the Bold and the New. Jeremy J. Siegel, Crown Business, New York, E-book at The Kindle Store, Amazon.com

"THE PRUDENT INVESTORS GUIDE TO BEATING THE MARKET". John J. Bowen, Jr., Carl H. Reinhardt, Alan B. Werba, Irwin Professional Publishing, Chicago 1996, ISBN: 0-7863-0365-4